8·99

WRITERS AND THEIR WORK

ISOBEL ARMSTRONG
General Editor

BRYAN LOUGHREY
Advisory Editor

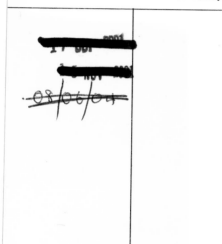

D1382505

CHRISTINA ROSSETTI

a portrait in coloured chalks on paper by Dante Gabriel Rossetti, 1877
Private Collection/National Portrait Gallery, London

CHRISTINA
ROSSETTI

KATHRYN BURLINSON

Northcote House
in association with the
British Council

First published in 1998 by Northcote House Publishers Ltd, Plymbridge House, Estover Road, Plymouth PL6 7PY, United Kingdom.
Tel: +44 (01752) 202368 Fax: +44 (01752) 202330.

British Library Cataloguing-in-Publication Data
A catalogue record for this book is available from the British Library

ISBN 0-7463-0846-9

Typeset by PDQ Typesetting, Newcastle-under-Lyme
Printed and bound in the United Kingdom

For Gemma,
and in memory of Pa

Contents

Acknowledgements

I would like to thank Isobel Armstrong for her support and her trenchant comments; she has always helped shape and sharpen my thinking about Rossetti. I also thank the British Academy and the University of Southampton for their financial support of my research. My time in the English Department at Southampton was made endlessly stimulating and enjoyable by both colleagues and students, who, in many different ways, challenged, excited, and inspired me. Thank you all.

I am very grateful to those who read the typescript: Aidan Day, Hugo Donnelly, Paul Hamilton, Lucy Hartley, Edmund Papst, and Nadia Valman generously offered responses and comments. I would also like to extend special thanks to Tony Harrison, for the wise counsel he offered when I really needed it.

Finally, I wish to express my love and gratitude to my mother and stepfather, Angela and Stan Wilcox, for their past generosity in helping me to continue studying. This book is, in part, dedicated to my stepfather's memory. But I wrote it for Gemma, my niece.

Biographical Outline

1826   Marriage of Frances Polidori and Gabriele Rossetti.

1827   Maria Francesca born.

1828   Dante Gabriel born.

1829   William Michael born.

1830   Christina Georgina born 5 December, 38 Charlotte St., London.

1835   Family move to 50 Charlotte St.

1842   Christina writes 'To my Mother on her Birthday'.

1843   Frances, Maria, and Christina start to attend Christ Church, Albany St.

1845   Christina's adolescent breakdown and illness begin.

1847   *Verses* privately published.

1848   Pre-Raphaelite Brotherhood (PRB) founded. 'Death's Chill Between' and 'Heart's Chill Between' published in the *Athenaeum*. CGR becomes engaged to James Collinson.

1850   Writes *Maude*. *The Germ* published with poems by CGR. Engagement to Collinson broken off following his reversion to Catholicism.

1851   CGR assists Frances in school-teaching. Family move to 38 Arlington St.

1852   Contributes Italian poems and unfinished epistolary novel *Corrispondenzia Famigliare* to *The Bouquet* (magazine established by a group of young women).

1853   CGR and Frances leave for Frome, Somerset, to open a school.

1854   Family move to 45 Albany St. Death of Gabriele Rossetti. CGR volunteers to become a nurse in the Crimea – refused because considered too young.

1859   Becomes a voluntary worker at St Mary Magdalene Penitentiary, Highgate. Writes *Goblin Market*. 'The Round

Tower at Jhansi: June 8 1857' and 'Maude Clare' published in *Once a Week*.

1860   Dante Gabriel marries Lizzie Siddal.

1861   'A Birthday' and 'Up-Hill' published in *Macmillan's Magazine*. Death of Elizabeth Barrett Browning.

1862   *Goblin Market and Other Poems* published to positive reviews. CGR begins close friendship with Charles Bagot Cayley. Travels with Frances and William to France. Lizzie Siddal dies from laudanum overdose.

1864   'The Lowest Room' published in *Macmillan's Magazine*.

1865   CGR, Frances, and William Michael travel in mainland Europe, including Italy.

1866   Publication of *The Prince's Progress and Other Poems*. 'Hero' published in *The Argosy*. Cayley proposes, CGR declines.

1867   Moves to 56 Euston Square with Frances, William Michael and aunts Eliza and Charlotte.

1870   *Commonplace and Other Short Stories* published. Health seriously deteriorates.

1871   In November first copies of *Sing-Song: A Nursery Rhyme Book* appear (dated 1872).

1872   CGR diagnosed as having Graves's disease (exophthalmic bronchole). Dante Gabriel's mental health deteriorates. He suffers paranoia and nervous collapse.

1873   Maria joins All Saints Sisterhood.

1874   *Speaking Likenesses* and *Annus Domini* published. William Michael marries Lucy Madox Brown.

1875   Publication of *Goblin Market, the Prince's Progress, and Other Poems*.

1876   CGR, Frances, and aunts Eliza and Charlotte move to 30 Torrington Square. Death of Maria Rossetti.

1879   *Seek and Find* published.

1881   *A Pageant, and Other Poems* and *Called to Be Saints* published.

1882   Death of Dante Gabriel Rossetti.

1883   *Letter and Spirit* published. Death of Charles Cayley.

1885   *Time Flies* published.

1886   Death of Frances Rossetti.

1890   Death of Aunt Charlotte.

1892   *The Face of the Deep* published. CGR has surgery for cancer.

1893   *Verses* published. Aunt Eliza dies.

1894   Death of Christina Rossetti, 29 December, from cancer.

Abbreviations and References

References to Christina Rossetti's poetry and prose are, where possible, to the widely available select edition *Christina Rossetti: Poems and Prose*, ed. Jan Marsh (London: Everyman, 1994). Other references are to *The Complete Poems of Christina Rossetti*, ed. R. W. Crump (3 vols.; Baton Rouge, La.: Louisiana State University Press, 1979–90) and to original prose editions. Where Marsh's transcription of poems differs from Crump's, Crump has been taken as authoritative, with the exception of 'Daydreams' and 'A Nightmare', where Marsh's text is used.

The following abbreviations have been used in citing works:

AD   *Annus Domini: A Prayer for Each Day of the Year* (London: James Parker, 1874)

CP   *The Complete Poems of Christina Rossetti: A Variorum Edition*, ed. R. W. Crump (3 vols.; Baton Rouge, La.: Louisiana State University Press, 1979–90)

FD   *The Face of the Deep: A Devotional Commentary on the Apocalypse* (London: SPCK, 1892)

FL   *The Family Letters of Christina Georgina Rossetti*, ed. W. M. Rossetti (London: Brown, Langham & Co., 1908).

LCR   *The Letters of Christina Rossetti*, ed. Antony H. Harrison (4 vols.; Charlottesville, Va.: University Press of Virginia, 1997–)

LS   *Letter and Spirit: Notes on the Commandments* (London: SPCK, 1883)

PP   *Christina Rossetti: Poems and Prose*, ed. Jan Marsh (London: Everyman, 1994)

PW   *The Poetical Works of Christina Georgina Rossetti with Memoir and Notes*, ed. W. M. Rossetti (London: Macmillan, 1904)

SF   *Seek and Find: A Double Series of Short Studies of the Benedicite* (London: SPCK, 1879)

TF   *Time Flies: A Reading Diary* (London: SPCK, 1885)

TR   *Three Rossettis: Unpublished Letters to and from Dante Gabriel, Christina, William*, ed. Janet Camp Troxell (Cambridge: Cambridge University Press, 1937)

Prologue

Christina Rossetti is a major poet of the nineteenth century. After decades of critical marginalization and neglect in the first half of the twentieth century, she is now widely recognized as a crucially important Victorian writer and one of the best women poets of all time. In a 1998 review of Victorian poetry in the *Times Literary Supplement*, Nicholas Shrimpton rightly comments on Rossetti's status, claiming that her 'elevation to the premier league is unmistakable'; she has moved 'firmly into the first rank.'[1]

This study does not dwell upon Rossetti's life, nor does it pay detailed attention to the Pre-Raphaelite sphere in which her art developed, since Jan Marsh's *Christina Rossetti: A Literary Biography* (1994) thoroughly pursues the connections between life and work and provides a wealth of information about the literary, artistic, and familial contexts in which her early writings were produced. Rather, this book focuses on three aspects of Rossetti's work primarily through readings of specific texts: Chapter 1, entitled 'Mind', examines the imaginative challenges involved in reading Rossetti and explores the unique ways in which she poses problems for interpreters. Her delight in language, her love of mystery, and her wry sense of humour are central to her art and it is these dispositions that the texts considered in this chapter conspicuously display. Chapter 2, 'Body', then turns to consider Rossetti as cultural critic, focusing upon the ways in which she writes about sexuality, women, and the body in Victorian culture. The representational indeterminacy and instability emphasized in Chapter 1 reappear in Chapter 2, but here 'dreaming through the twilight' is modified by sustained attention to social concerns and an attendant, irrepressible desire to break the silence and speak out.

In the final chapter of this book – 'Spirit' – I turn to Rossetti's devotional writings and to the ways that, even in apparently orthodox religious poetry and prose, extraordinary and unpredictable turns occur. As with any literary form or tradition that she encountered, from the sonnet to the fairy tale, from seventeenth-century poetry to Romanticism, in her devotional work Rossetti subtly, quietly, alters conventional interpretations, pretending as so often, that she is doing nothing of the kind. 'Far be it from me...', she declares, in typically modest, unassuming rhetoric – rhetoric which only now, more than a century after her death, is being recognized as Rossetti's deftly woven self-protection and self-disguise: her best-kept secret and the best language-game of all.

1

Mind

'I tell my secret? No indeed, not I:'

('Winter: My Secret' (*PP* 62, l. 1))

Christina Rossetti is one of the most strategic, secretive, and mysterious of poets. As such, she is one of the most intriguing. She is fascinated by 'The mystery of Life, the mystery | Of Death' ('Mirrors of Life and Death' (*CP* ii. 75, ll. 1–2)), and her work deliberately cultivates uncertainty and enigma; it is slippery and elusive, sometimes flagrantly refusing to offer stability of meaning or to conform to rational paradigms. 'What can it mean? you ask. I answer not | For meaning...', declares the playful, contrary speaker of 'My Dream' (*PP* 41, ll. 49–50).

Rossetti's imagination is drawn to the world of dreams and daydreams, to indeterminate states of consciousness that exist at the edges, the borders, the thresholds of the known. Her imagination ignores conventional time frames: unlike many fellow Victorians, whose religious faith was challenged by earlier geological discoveries revealing the biblical version of creation to be erroneous, Rossetti maintained absolute trust in the power of the divine and above all in its unknowable nature. The seven days of creation, she argues, should not be understood literally, but symbolically, as 'lapses of time by us unmeasured and immeasurable' (*SF* 87). The seventh day, furthermore, may not be finished, but 'still in progress, still incomplete', thus, 'All the earth becomes holy ground' (*SF* 89–90).

Rossetti believed from an early age that as mortal bodies we see through a glass darkly, a perspective encouraged by Tractarian teachings, to which Rossetti was directly exposed from the age of 12, when she, her mother, and her sister, Maria, began to attend services at Christ Church, Albany St.[1] The idea

1

that the visible world typifies the invisible was a perspective that she maintained throughout her life. In her last major prose work, *The Face of the Deep* (1892), she writes that, 'matter suggests the immaterial; time eternity... the literal are no more than types of the spiritual' (FD 215, 238). Such an imaginative connection to dimensions beyond the material is evident especially in poems such as 'After Death' and 'At Home' (PP 22, 64), texts that venture into the afterlife and speak back to the world from that necessarily unfathomable space. Elsewhere, Rossetti repeatedly emphasizes the limitations of earthly perceptions, often by recourse to Isaiah 64: 4 and 1 Corinthians 2: 9: 'Eye hath not seen, nor ear hath heard, nor heart conceived.' But despite her recognition of the problems of representing the noumenal, Rossetti's textual strategies still encourage her readers to travel with her to the farthest boundaries of what can be depicted and, as far as possible beyond that, to the ineffable.

In a lesser poet, such a cast of mind might result in work that is vague, undisciplined, or uncontrolled. But Rossetti's work is not like this. It is rigorously crafted. From a very young age, she demonstrated a sophisticated understanding of form and clearly took great pleasure in making language work within the demands of particular poetic constraints. Christina was the youngest of four children born to Italian emigré Gabriele Rossetti and to Anglo-Italian Frances Polidori, but her relative immaturity did not prevent her from competing enthusiastically with her brothers and sister in games of *bouts rimés*, in which the final word of each line of a sonnet is given and the rest must be composed. Rossetti thus learned her craft early: in 1847, when she was 16, a collection of her verses showing notable command of poetic form was published by her grandfather, Gaetano Polidori.

SECRET SELVES

As well as possessing precocious talent, intense imagination, and mystical vision, Rossetti displayed a keen self-consciousness from an early age – a quality that affects all forms of self-representation in her work. Despite being described by her father as, temperamentally, one of the 'two storms' of the family (her gifted brother Dante Gabriel was the other, while Maria and William Michael were the 'two calms'), Rossetti was shy in company and, though ambitious, reticent about her work. The public display of talent or achievement was widely thought to be inappropriate for Victorian girls, so Rossetti was in a difficult position as both a young woman and a writer. Outwardly manifesting extreme modesty was one way to offset potential criticism, if not to resolve the internal conflict of social and artistic interests. In her early, semi-autobiographical novella, *Maude* (written in 1850), the split between private and public selves is evident from the first page. 'A penny for your thoughts,' asks Maude's mother, but the offer is not taken up. Instead, while her mother chatters about social engagements, Maude 'slip[s] out of sight some scrawled paper' and locks her writing book, giving nothing away (*PP* 252).

By writing about the young poet's scribbled secrets, Rossetti effectively exposes the existence of those secrets to her reading public. Subsequently, and similarly, we are told that Maude's 'original compositions' are 'not intended for the public eye' (*PP* 252), yet in the very next sentence we are presented with a sonnet written by Maude. Such paradoxical representation dramatizes feminine dilemmas – a strategy Rossetti uses to great effect in many early texts. Despite such dramatization, however, we are not told the actual secrets of the young artist herself. Maude's finished sonnet is not the scrawled paper; the remaining contents of her writing book and of Maude's mind and heart remain locked from view. The wish for self-exposure competes with an even stronger desire for self-protection.

Rossetti plays with the dynamic of exposing Maude and keeping her hidden throughout the story. The young poet's work and its relation to her personality is deliberately depicted as a puzzle. In referring to the range of critical interpretations brought to bear on Maude's writing, Rossetti, through the voice of the narrator, demonstrates her awareness of her own inscrutability to others. In her narratorial role she also exhibits a characteristic evasiveness about what causes such impenetrability:

> Touching these same verses, it was the amazement of everyone what could make her poetry so broken-hearted as was mostly the case. Some pronounced that she wrote very foolishly about things she could not possibly understand; some wondered if she really had any secret source of uneasiness; while some simply set her down as

affected. Perhaps there was a degree of truth in all these opinions. (*PP* 253)

'Perhaps...a degree of truth....' Even in the narrator's gesture towards elucidation, we find a reluctance to provide readers with a secure interpretative foothold. The narrator's strategy is to keep possibilities open, to keep us guessing not just about Maude, but about the validity of and motives behind our own critical speculations. By denying us access to Maude's secrets, we are prevented from fixing readings and kept in a state of suspension. Implicitly, we are asked to accept that responses are always subjective, provisional, and do not constitute absolute truths. Although Dante Gabriel Rossetti ridiculed his sister for giving a poem the title 'Something Like Truth' (later changed to 'Sleep at Sea' (*CP* i. 79)),[2] this was quite in keeping with tendencies exhibited elsewhere in Christina's apparently pellucid, but actually opaque and elusive work.

States of uncertainty are registered, too, in poems concerned with self-exploration. In 'Day-Dreams' (*PP* 55), written in 1857, the speaker ponders the mysteries of her own soul, asking 'Who can guess or read her will?' (l. 15):

> Is it love she looks and longs for,
>   Is it rest or peace,
> Is it slumber self-forgetful
>   In its utter ease,
> Is it one or all of these?

(ll. 21–5)

No revelation occurs in the poem; the speaker even becomes sceptical about whether her enquiry is worthwhile: 'Now if I could guess her secret | Were it worth the guess? –' (ll. 41–2). The very last line of the poem, 'While I wondered what she meant' (l. 55), leaves both speaker and reader in limbo, as a mood of resignation to the soul's obscurity outstrips the initial desire for clarity.

In a much later composition, and in the context of relationship to another person rather than to the self, we again find a marked emphasis on the unpredictable. The speaker of 'Touching "Never"' (*CP* ii. 102) begins her address with the query, 'Because you never yet have loved me, dear, | Think you you never can nor ever will?' (ll. 1–2). The instability of human

4

feelings, their flux and flow, makes the speaker propose emotional flexibility as the most preferable stance when speaking of love. She concludes her argument with her apparently unbending friend by declaring that, if the positions of the two were reversed, she would be receptive to potential changes of feeling. This is cast in a typical mixture of assertion and reserve: 'I would have owned the point you pressed on me, | Was possible, or probable, or true' (ll. 13–14).

It is possible, probable, or true that Maude writes about things she does not understand, has a secret source of uneasiness and/or is merely affected. The speculations about the soul in 'Day-Dreams' are similarly valid: she could be seeking peace, romance, or release, 'knowledge, love, or pride' (l. 35). The self and all its relations are unstable: in 'Love attacked' (*CP* iii. 86), a juvenile poem included in the 1847 collection, Rossetti wrote of human love as essentially 'fleeting' (l. 11), a view she maintained, although she uses it to defend love's vicissitudes in 'Touching "Never"'. The important thing is that, for Rossetti, everything that exists in the phenomenal world is mutable: nature, individuals, societies, feelings. As such, it is no place for rigidity.

In *Seek and Find* (1879), Rossetti emphasizes that 'This present temporal stage of our existence is a stage of possibilities, alternatives, hope, fear: that word "never" belongs to our next eternal stage' (*SF* 102). So we abide in a world of 'perhaps', and it is from this indefinite point that Rossetti frequently writes. In one of her most famous lyrics, 'When I am dead, my dearest' (*PP* 18), the speaker concludes her song in a manner that leaves eschatological questions tantalizingly open:

> And dreaming through the twilight
>   That doth not rise nor set,
> Haply I may remember,
>   And haply may forget.

(ll. 13–16)

Just as twilight, one of Rossetti's favourite temporal locations, is an indefinite time between day and night, 'perhaps' lies between certainty and uncertainty and is, by definition, impossible to fix. Rossetti's poetry frequently has the effect not only of generating, but also of extending our sense of uncertainty beyond familiar boundaries, whether she is dealing with the mysteries of individuals or with dimensions entirely beyond the knowledge of the living. Such indeterminacy and epistemological caution, furthermore, are woven into the texture and form of the verse itself.[3]

Rossetti's interest both in the problems of understanding and interpretation, and in formal exploration, is evident throughout her work. Although known primarily as a lyric poet, she ranges widely in her use of genre, writing sonnets and ballads, narrative and devotional poetry, nursery rhymes, fairy tales, short stories, dramatic monologues, a novella, and several books of devotional prose (which, although relatively ignored in criticism, earned Rossetti more money and a wider readership than any of her poetry). In devotional works such as *Seek and Find* and *The Face of the Deep*, it is the author herself who practises interpretation, despite her own acknowledgement that she is entering a mysterious textual maze: 'which verse of the Holy Bible may not veil a mystery?' (*FD* 92).

To engage in theology or biblical exegesis, however, was seen by many Victorians to be beyond woman's ability or place, so Rossetti's readings of biblical texts are often framed by disclaimers and apologias, such as 'To expound prophecy lies of course beyond my power, and not within my wish' (*FD* 195). Such gestures towards convention are, however, undermined by the alternative and even radical interpretations of orthodox theological perspectives offered, particularly where issues of gender are at stake. These will be examined in more detail in Chapter 3, but I draw attention to this body of work here not only because it illustrates a characteristic blend of genuinely felt modesty and firm self-assurance, but also because it demonstrates a tendency, despite apparent deference to masculine authority, to refuse any human being the right to claim access to absolute knowledge. 'Be it...as seems indeed indisputable, that certain things are and must remain positively and permanently inferior: it may still transcend our present faculties to decide authoritatively which is which' (*SF* 63–4). Judgement, in Rossetti's view, is not by man, but by God; people have only 'partial knowledge' (*SF* 116) and if we cannot say 'never', neither can we say 'always'. The voice of Rossetti's devotional prose advises 'men as are tyrannical and oppressive' to 'searchings of spirit' (*AD* 19), emphasizing throughout her work that arrogant claims to truth are inadvisable and a greater judgement than that of humankind awaits. In the context of high Victorian culture, Rossetti's work offers a profound criticism of those who, without hesitation, claim the right to expound.

Rossetti's questioning of the process, ethics, and consequences of interpretation surfaces in her manipulation of generic forms as well as in the explicit content of her writing. Her use of fairy-tale structures and motifs coexists with formal revisions which upset conventional expectations of stable morals or transparent allegories. 'The Prince's Progress', the title poem of Rossetti's 1866 collection, undermines the conventions of the masculine quest as well as revising the fairy tale of Sleeping Beauty – one of the nineteenth century's most enduring and popular stories. 'The Prince's Progress' is also a poem about the perils of interpretation: the prince misreads or fails to respond to the symbolic signs around him, with fatal results for his beloved object of desire, who dies before he reaches her bedside.[4]

That many of Rossetti's texts show themselves to be concerned with interpretation, inviting it, questioning it, refusing it, has proved highly attractive to literary and cultural critics since the late 1970s, when feminist, post-structuralist, and historicist readings have been overwhelmingly influential and patriarchal precedent constantly called into question. One of Rossetti's most notorious works, the sensually outrageous *Goblin Market* (1862), has provoked innumerable commentators to ponder its mysteries, to attempt to find the key to the sumptuous but disturbing fairy tale of Laura, Lizzie, and the goblins.[5] The poem's paradoxes and ambiguities puzzle and intrigue readers today just as they did contemporary reviewer Caroline Norton, who claims the poem 'is one of the works which are said to "defy criticism". Is it a fable – or a mere fairy story – or an allegory against the pleasures of sinful love – or what is it?'[6] Over a century later, at a time when second-wave feminist critics were starting to reclaim the work of earlier women writers, Germaine Greer wrote in an introduction to the poem that '*Goblin Market* will, like Christina Rossetti herself, keep its secret forever' (*PP* 469). This is possible, or probable, or true, but Greer's statement nevertheless presupposes a core secret, a kernel of absolute meaning or explanation that *Goblin Market* particularly and Rossetti's work generally contest. Perhaps it

7

would be wise to recall lines from Rossetti's well-known poem 'Winter: My Secret' to keep our alternatives open:

> Or, after all, perhaps there's none:
> Suppose there is no secret after all,
> But only just my fun.

(ll. 7–9)

Rossetti's quirky and teasing sense of humour defies the common image of her as an ailing Victorian spinster with a predilection for morbidity. Whilst it is apt to comment, as did Virginia Woolf in her perceptive piece 'I am Christina Rossetti', that 'Death, oblivion and rest lap round your songs with their dark wave', it is also true, as Woolf recognized, that Rossetti 'pulled legs' and 'tweaked noses' (*PP* 467). The poet's dry and often acid wit surfaces in poetry and letters alike. In correspondence with her brothers, she is ironical and self-mocking, likening her 'sparkling self' to a local inn – 'The Blue Boar' – and speaking of her poems as 'groans' (*LCR* i. 62, Letter 47; i. 348, Letter 416). Rossetti's awareness of her own poetic self-fashioning warns us once again not to assume we have the measure of her, any more than we should be deluded into believing that the 'simple surfaces' of her poetry make the poems simplistic. It is only in recent years that Rossetti's sheer intellect has begun to be appreciated and that the image passed down to us via William Michael's representation of his sister as 'casual and spontaneous' in composition and erratically read has been overturned (*PW*, pp. lxviii–lxix).[7] She is now seen as one of the most important Victorian poets, appreciated especially for her revisions of literary texts and traditions from Petrarch and Dante through the seventeenth-century poets, to the Romantics and her own contemporary Victorians. Such willingness to engage in intertextual debate with her predominantly male, highly renowned forebears testifies to her underlying confidence in her own ability with both form and ideas and defies her publicly self-deprecating persona.

FLIRTING

Rossetti exerts confidence, too, in the way that her speakers indulge in flirtatious play with readers, provoking and teasing us into efforts of understanding and then leaving us floating in uncertainty. 'Winter: My Secret' and 'My Dream', both written during a highly productive period for Rossetti in the 1850s, are poems that refuse to reveal secrets or to explain dreams. Their beguiling explorations are particularly susceptible to psycho-analytic critical analysis; above all they exploit the reader's wish to 'know'. After refusing to answer for meaning in 'My Dream', the speaker throws the question back: 'I answer not | For meaning, but myself must echo, What?' (ll. 49–50). This refusal of the poem to offer explanation undermines the reader's desire to secure his or her subjectivity in relation to the text. The desire *'to give meaning'* is, according to Julia Kristeva, an epistemolo-gical attitude which is 'not innocent but, rather, is rooted in the speaking subject's need to reassure himself of his image and his identity faced with an object'.[8] Such reassurance is not easy to find in Rossetti, but her challenge to her readers does not consist in a negation of interpretative desire, rather in how we choose to respond to the echoing back to us of the impulse to critical enquiry itself.

Let us look in detail at how this works in 'My Dream', a poem that ostensibly recounts a dream about a ravenous crocodile who devours his smaller kin. In its opening lines, the poem raises a series of difficulties concerning the position of the speaker and the relationship she establishes with the reader:

> Hear now a curious dream I dreamed last night,
> Each word whereof is weighed and sifted truth.
>
> (ll. 1–2)

The combination, in the opening line, of the injunction to the reader and the reference to a dream places us in a position of some intimacy. There is a sense of privilege as the speaker states that the dream is recent – this is, it suggests, fresh psychic material, ripe for interpretative activity. Yet such intimacy and immediacy are qualified by the text's second line, where we are informed that the representation of the dream in words has been carefully considered. We are made aware of the process of linguistic selection and omission (or secondary revision) that has occurred between the dream and its conscious reconstruction.[9] Furthermore, we are assured that what we are about to hear is

9

carefully considered 'truth' – a claim that asserts the veracity of the speaker's mediated version of the dream, but may put us on our guard if we bear in mind Rossetti's tendency to highlight the partial nature of secular claims to absolute truth. In its opening couplet, then, 'My Dream' both beckons and resists interpretation, seducing the reader with the promise of strangeness and holding him or her back by emphasizing mediation and strategic representation. This calls attention to, indeed demands, that the hermeneutic process be reflected upon.

The self-sifted dream then commences and for the first six lines we read of a swelling pregnant Euphrates river giving birth to a host of young crocodiles. The tale is at that point interrupted by an interjection that calls attention to the reader–speaker relationship:

> The rest if I should tell, I fear my friend,
> My closest friend would deem the facts untrue;
> And therefore it were wisely left untold;
> Yet if you will, why, hear it to the end.

(ll. 9–12)

We now encounter anxiety regarding the reader's willingness to accept the tale. The speaker is still insisting that her story is true, but she is tentative – a seductive strategy, in so far as we are figured as especially intimate, as closer than the closest friend if we choose to accept the authenticity of the dream text. No sooner are we drawn in, however, than we are casually rebuffed. Indifference follows intimacy, as if we are caught in a dynamic of transference where the terms of desire for or rejection of the other are being dictated, unpredictably, by the individual undergoing analysis. This is not to suggest that there is no difference between a literary text and a person in therapy, nor to ignore the fact that 'My Dream' predates psychoanalysis, but it is to follow through the structural similarity in interpretative activity.

Wisely or not, we read on and encounter the terrifying king crocodile, a bejewelled and fearsome beast, whose chest gleams with polished stones in the shapes of 'crowns and orbs and sceptres' (l. 17), whereupon the narrative is again interrupted. 'But who shall tell the tale of all their woes?' (l. 24), asks the speaker, disingenuously, since she is the only possible narrator of this private tale. The speaker draws attention to the power of her position as she implicitly alerts us to her own identity as storyteller, emphasizing the act of writing and, again, the fact that this story is mediated.

The reflexive concern with storytellers and their power is a recurring feature of Rossetti's writings, coming particularly to the fore in *Goblin Market* and in the shockingly violent children's story, *Speaking Likenesses* (PP 324), where the apparently proper, upstanding narrator, 'Aunt', wields her narrative power in such devious and manipulative ways that, ultimately, she manifests in her own discourse many of the faults she ascribes to the hideous characters in the story-within-the-story.[10] Suffice to say that Rossetti is as interested in ways of telling stories as in stories themselves, as is abundantly clear in the example of 'My Dream'.

If there are moments in 'My Dream' where the speaker seems willing to accept an interpretative or guiding role, in a final volte-face at the end of the poem she rejects responsibility as co-producer of meaning:

> What can it mean? you ask. I answer not
> For meaning, but myself must echo, What?
> And tell it as I saw it on the spot.

(ll. 49–51

Just as Rossetti denied that she meant anything important in *Goblin Market*, leaving readers free to interpret as they will, so here the speaker throws the question of meaning back to the reader. As Rossetti's friend Lewis Carroll recognized in responding to a similar question about meaning, authorial intention cannot entirely predict or control reception: 'As to the meaning of the *Snark*? I'm very much afraid I didn't mean anything but nonsense! Still, you know, words mean more than we mean to express when we use them'.[11]

One option for Rossetti's readers is to accept her challenge, to attempt to decipher the images of 'My Dream', to read them symbolically or allegorically, to produce an alternative narrative. But while such interpretative desire may be irresistible, to indulge it is to play into the hands of one who knows she teases. As in other Victorian texts categorized as literary nonsense, Rossetti is here presenting her readers with a riddle which cannot be answered. Just as it is futile to ponder with Alice why a raven is like a writing desk, since the riddle, outrageously, has no solution, so it appears that in 'My Dream' we are but patched fools if we try to decipher bottomless dreams. Any such endeavour is further robbed of ultimate significance when Rossetti writes next to the poem in her own 1875 edition: 'not a real dream' (PW 479).

This authorial note adds a further layer of mystery and strengthens the argument that the poem is as much preoccupied with hermeneutical questions as with the representation of a vision. It seems to delight in its own impenetrability, teasing us into interpretative gestures that may ultimately seem fantastical or even risible. For some, this strategy provokes irritation. William Michael Rossetti claims in his memoir of his sister that the poem illustrates Christina's 'exceptional turn of mind...the odd freakishness which flecked the extreme and almost excessive seriousness of her thought'. He retreats from providing a reading, however: 'As it was not a real dream, and she chose nevertheless to give it verbal form, one seeks for a meaning in it, and I for one cannot find any that bears development' (PW 479).

William Michael's apparent frustration highlights a conventional form of investment in interpretative mastery. He wants to find 'a meaning' and dislikes the suggestive, provisional, and enigmatic that do not in the end offer epistemological security. Such rationally based objections might be identified as typically masculinist in stance, except that women commentators have been just as keen to uncover or unlock textual meaning. There is much to excite feminist readers in 'My Dream': following the hatching of the eggs from 'myriad pregnant waves' (l. 6), a male crocodile becomes 'lord and master of his kin' (l. 23) and proceeds to devour his 'punier brethren' (l. 21) in a frenzy of crunching and sucking. When he is 'gorged to the full' (l. 33) he physically shrinks: 'In sleep he dwindled to the common size' (l. 36).

It is easy to seize upon the phallic suggestiveness of the tyrannical crocodile; in recent years he has been interpreted as various members of the Pre-Raphaelite Brotherhood (PRB), as the Tzar of Russia, and as 'the Male in general'.[12] The crocodile, as well as having literary antecedents in the writings of Thomas De Quincey, is one of Rossetti's 'tyrannical and oppressive' masculine figures whom she likes to undermine. The croc is like

Kronos, a law unto himself, but he gets his inevitable come-uppance near the end of the poem, following the appearance of an avenging 'wingèd vessel' (l. 38). The suggestion of the crocodile's physical shrinking might produce a smirk after the aggressive masculinist behaviour of the reptile 'lord and master', but it is also significant that in this moment 'all the empire' (l. 37) on the crocodile's 'coat' disappears too. The Crimean context in which the poem was written may justify an allegorical interpretation of the crocodile as Russia's Tzar and the avenging vessel as British troops, but a historicist reading such as this has also to be set against the equally justifiable suggestion of Christian allegory in which pagan energies are displaced by the civilizing mission of the avenging vessel which levels the waters of the Euphrates. Both readings may be pursued to suggest that an ideological move occurs in the poem so that God and right are seen to be on Britain's side, but this idea remains so undeveloped in the poem that it is not finally persuasive or satisfying. As in *Goblin Market*, there is a surfeit of interpretative possibilities, all of which, individually or collectively, fall short of explaining the imaginative power and comical play that are so central to the poem's overall signification.

As Cora Kaplan shrewdly comments, 'My Dream' is 'a jokey lesson to critical head-hunters tracking either phalluses, patriarchs or oppressors, or all three'.[13] Kaplan's emphasis on the poem's comedy acts as a useful warning to overzealous psychoanalytically inclined readers, though the textual combination of sexuality, dreams, and jokes does connect in intriguing ways with Freud's work. In his 'Introductory Lecture' on dreams, Freud cites 'instances in which it has been far from easy to decide whether what we are dealing with is a joke or a dream'.[14] 'My Dream' certainly possesses the double-sidedness or duplicity in language that Freud anchors to the psychical structure of jokes, as well as suggesting condensation and displacement–features shared by both jokes and dreams.[15]

But 'My Dream' also highlights the structures we use to read language and exposes the fantasies therein. It is a fantasy text that is addressing the poetics of fantasy. Representing a 'dream' text for consumption and interpretation asks a double question about meaning, for the speaker is unsure whether she has an object that can be made to mean (the dream's fictional status notwithstanding). It is this problem – or this joke – that she presents to the reader, except that we cannot address this particular problem, since interposed between us and the 'dream' – the phantasmatic origin – is the mediated text. This, however, is of course the problem for the speaker as well. She cannot know whether her 'dream' can 'mean' because, for one thing, her writing is a retrospective reconstruction of a questionable source. Writing has inflicted a change upon the dream material, and, although it is unknowable without language, it is inevitably distorted by it. 'My Dream' is then not my dream at all – it is not knowable to me.

'My Dream' is an exceptionally playful and testing poem, but it may legitimately be grouped with other texts that share its sense of fun while raising seriously challenging questions. 'Winter: My Secret' is a poem so quintessentially Rossettian in strategy that it has been described by Isobel Armstrong as 'almost a summa' of the poet's work (*PP* 475). We are teased throughout the text with the suggestion of a secret, but, as in 'Day-Dreams', warned that there may not be a secret after all, 'but only just my fun' ('Winter: My Secret', 1.9). '[F]un', says Angela Carter, 'is pleasure without guilt',[16] which is precisely what Rossetti's speakers seem to experience in these provocative, flirtatious poems. The tactics Rossetti uses not only make the game she is playing uncertain, but make uncertainty the game, and here her work chimes with the interpretation of flirting offered by psychoanalyst Adam Phillips, who claims it to be the 'calculated production of uncertainty', which 'does not make a virtue of instability, but a pleasure'.[17]

The first line of 'Winter: My Secret' is structured flirtatiously, ensuring maximum attraction and resistance. It is symmetrical, flanked on both ends by identical guard-posts that are also the guardians of identity: 'I tell my secret? No indeed, not I:' (l. 1).[18] Both 'I' and 'not I' are implicated in the textual exploration as the poem plays with the reader's desire to make meaning. The poem's first line opens the possibility of telling and then snaps shut. The second opens once more, but into a now-familiar rhetoric of indeterminacy: 'Perhaps some day, who knows?' (l. 2). Locating meaning in subjective and temporal codes is raised as a possibility, only to be subsequently resisted:

> But not today; it froze, and blows, and snows,
> And you're too curious: fie!
> You want to hear it? well:
> Only, my secret's mine, and I won't tell.

(ll. 3–6)

The speaker surrounds herself with language, with lists of items and verbs, wrapping herself up as she plays with the idea of self-exposure. Her language moves metamorphically, especially in the list of internally and end-rhyming words in line 3: 'froze ... blows .. snows', where a flirtatious playing for time is enacted, repetition and reproduction run in parallel, closure is resisted, and difference kept in play.[19] The same formal technique is repeated later in the poem, when seven descriptive participles are attributed to the 'draughts' (l. 14) which threaten to nip and bite through the speaker's protective layers:

> Today's a nipping day, a biting day;
> In which one wants a shawl,
> A veil, a cloak, and other wraps:
> I cannot ope to every one who taps,
> And let the draughts come whistling thro' my hall;
> Come bounding and surrounding me,
> Come buffeting, astounding me,
> Nipping and clipping thro' my wraps and all.

(ll. 10–17)

The draughts seem to whip up their own momentum, while the speaker takes pleasure in the sound-play, rhythm, and rhymes that deviate from the conversational register of the poem as a whole. As in much Victorian nonsense writing, sound-play predominates over sense-play, and, since 'Nonsense' was Rossetti's original manuscript title for the poem, such a context is directly relevant.

Yet the poem is unlike other Victorian nonsense texts in the ways in which it suggests the possibility of a real secret that may be a key to understanding. Nonsense might invite readers to interpret, but it tends not to suggest that deeper meanings can be discovered.[20] Rossetti on the other hand, holds two possibilities in absolute balance: the secret is posited as the site both of ultimate truth and of ultimate deception. Even knowing this, there is a perpetual temptation to be a 'nipping', 'biting' reader and to try to strip the speaker of her 'veil ...

15

cloak, and other wraps'. We are 'curious' because, and only because, the poem deliberately cultivates our curiosity.

Rossetti uses a similar technique in another, very little discussed poem entitled, simply, 'What?' (*CP* iii. 214). 'What?' predates 'Winter: My Secret' – the former was written in 1853, the latter in 1857 – but in its persistent withholding of a central object it is comparable. The text lacks a main noun and consists of a series of metaphors that, though suggestive, reveal no ultimate referent. The signifying practice is constructed precisely around lack and absence. I quote the poem in full, since it does not appear in select editions:

> Strengthening as secret manna,
> Fostering as clouds above,
> Kind as a hovering dove,
> Full as a plenteous river,
> Our glory and our banner
> For ever and for ever.
>
> Dear as a dying cadence
> Of music in the drowsy night;
> Fair as the flowers which maidens
> Pluck for an hour's delight,
> And then forget them quite.
>
> Gay as a cowslip meadow
> Fresh opening to the sun
> When new day is begun;
> Soft as a sunny shadow
> When day is almost done.
>
> Glorious as purple twilight,
> Pleasant as budding tree,
> Untouched as any islet
> Shrined in an unknown sea;
> Sweet as a fragrant rose amid the dew; –
> As sweet, as fruitless too.
>
> A bitter dream to wake from,
> But oh how pleasant while we dream;
> A poisoned fount to take from,
> But oh how sweet the stream.

(ll. 1–26)

'What?' indeed. The metaphors suggest concerns with love, sexuality, masturbation, worldly pleasure, poetic language, but

'Is it one or all of these?' ('Day-Dreams', l. 25). The poem makes 'My Dream' seem accessible by comparison. 'What?' challenges us by its title but refuses us 'entry': we cannot 'get in' but are cast along from one line to the next, anticipating an epiphany that never occurs. We find abundance and decay, pleasure and guilt, betrayal and nurturing, but is it possible to say more than that?

It is a poem that speaks more through its silence than its language, and, though by no means alone in this, it is a particularly extreme example of its kind. The water imagery and references to flowers and to that which is 'Untouched' and 'unknown' suggest sexual possibility; this is compounded by the anxiety that seems to accompany pleasure. But tempting as it is to pursue such a reading, the textual strategy of this poem encourages us to be tentative in unleashing interpretative yearning, not least to avoid the *impasse* of hermeneutic circularity. Rossetti's poetry is often highly self-conscious about the ways in which writing, while apparently marking that which is desired, reinscribes the loss and absence it seeks to overcome. Just as the speaker of 'Three Stages' (*PP* 37) recognizes that there is no real substance to that which she ultimately desires: 'It is an empty name | I long for' (ll. 13–14), so the speaker of 'What?' seems to realize that some unspeakable, irrecoverable loss underpins everything she says.

In her impressive 1994 biography of Christina Rossetti, Jan Marsh suggests that the 'dark secret' at the heart of Rossetti's life was that she was a victim of sexual abuse, most likely perpetrated by her father. Marsh substantiates her argument by recourse to recent socio-psychological research, demonstrating that Rossetti uses in her work many of the same strategies of concealment as do survivors of incest.[21] But intriguing as Marsh's reading is, and even allowing that her thesis is possible, probable, or true, it suffers from the same flaw as all interpretations which seek to uncover and expose a core meaning. It inevitably plays down the extent to which Rossetti's dissimulation, however personally motivated, is an aesthetic strategy and one which was carefully cultivated and developed in response to a whole range of cultural, historical and ideological forces. Rossetti's aesthetic influences alone are diverse, and all contribute in different ways to her characteristically terse poetry. Pre-Raphaelite and Ruskinian, Neoplatonic and Augustinian, Tractarian, Dantean, and Petrarchan influences are all clearly heard, to name but those most usually identified as shaping her poetic development.[22] Rossetti's response to the ideologies of Romanticism, her relation to traditions of women's writing, and her sense of her own contemporary culture are also highly significant. Rossetti's secretive and fantastical poetry is, whatever else it may also be, a form of cultural intervention and cultural commentary.

The period during which Rossetti wrote the poems under discussion was one in which secrets filled the literary market place. Many of the most popular texts of the mid-nineteenth century are structured around mysteries or secrets that are revealed in the course of the narrative. Charlotte Brontë, Charles Dickens, and Elizabeth Gaskell all make use of the device; Wilkie Collins's and Mary Braddon's sensation novels *The Woman in White* and *Lady Audley's Secret* (both of which were serialized prior to their publication in the early 1860s) depend upon a core secret to which all other events in the narratives ultimately relate. Secrets appear in poetry, too: Browning's monologues in *The Ring and the Book* (1868–9) turn on the unknown motivation behind a murder, while Tennyson's 'Morte d'Arthur' (1842) and later his *Idylls of the King* (1859–85) make poetic use of the secret, adulterous relationship of Launcelot and Guinevere.

What is notable in Rossetti's handling of the topic is her refusal to provide readers with the pleasurable satisfaction of having discovered the secret. She uses the Tractarian aesthetic of reserve, but has fun with it, as if she has everything so under control that she can afford to play dangerous games. If an aspect of the Victorian preoccupation with secrets is a tacit recognition that the public codes of propriety concealed alternative and less wholesome forms of conduct, Rossetti's textual strategies hover between, and play with, propriety and impropriety alike. This is not to suggest that she takes neither one seriously (in fact the opposite is the case), but to argue that she is taking familiar models of representation and looking at them from a different angle – one which functions as a kind of meta-narrative on wider cultural and literary preoccupations.

RIDDLE AND RHYME

Rossetti's work of the 1850s also develops the sub-genre of poetic riddles that had its heyday in the Renaissance but was enduringly popular with women writers of the eighteenth and nineteenth centuries. Some of Rossetti's earliest published pieces – the anagrams 'New Enigmas' and 'Charades' (*CP* iii. 24, 25) published in *Marshall's Ladies Daily Remembrancer* (1850) – work directly within the tradition: they are riddles that have answers provided the reader can decode the language-game. A feature of this kind of writing is its indulgence in linguistic playfulness: riddles, together with their generic relatives acrostics, anagrams, and nursery rhymes, are experiments with sound and pattern as well as sense. As such, they appeal to Rossetti. Throughout her life she was fond of riddles: as a child she was familiar with publications such as Batchelar's *Pleasant Exercises for Little Minds* (1820), and as late as 1886 she invented a riddle for her nephew Arthur (William Michael's son) and sent it to him in a letter.[23]

Poems such as 'Winter: My Secret' develop out of this riddle tradition, as does a body of work Rossetti produced specifically for children. Her acclaimed *Sing-Song* (1872) collection of nursery rhymes and children's verse includes poems such as 'A city plum is not a plum', 'A pin has a head, but has no hair', 'There is one that has a head without an eye', and 'The peacock has a score of eyes' (*CP* ii. 21, 32, 36; *PP* 135). Such poems stick quite closely to the forms found in works such as the *Book of merrie Riddles* (1631); one feature of such riddles is that they illustrate the multiple applications of words to things. Equally illustrated is the instability of language, its contextually determined meaning rather than its stable referents: 'A sailor's cat is not a cat', Rossetti informs us in 'A city plum . . .' (l. 4) and, in the same poem, the word 'bell' does not refer to an actual bell, but to a dumb-bell, which is 'no bell, though dumb' (l. 2). In such riddles, signifiers are not coincident with signifieds. Learning to work out the riddles or realize the referents is enjoyable, because the reader has the satisfaction of finding a meaning, but simultaneously the poems have fun with readers by exploiting the dissociation and estrangement that metaphor can bring to literal discourse.

Elsewhere in the nursery rhymes of the *Sing-Song* collection, Rossetti's assured handling of form, together with her far-reaching imagination, combine to make her contribution to this field of women's writing outstanding. Nursery rhymes are conventionally constructed around simple or comical rhymes that function mnemonically. As well as being used to entertain, they encourage language acquisition by teaching the pleasures of repetition. They delight in the sound-play provided by duplicated syllables, and their often nonsensical content allows children to focus on the euphonic aspects of language. At the same time, however, the use of fantasy helps to order experience by upsetting conventional structures so that these structures may be more clearly apprehended.

Rossetti's *Sing-Song* rhymes are influenced by earlier women's publications, such as Jane and Ann Taylor's landmark *Rhymes for the Nursery* (1806), or her friend Mary Howitt's mid-century productions, but they also, as do other texts so far considered, bear comparison with Victorian nonsense verse, especially when they play not just with sound but with rules. Reversals and inversions, repetition, arbitrariness, puns, and lists are formal features that are complemented by explorations of the relation between structure and semantics.

> If a pig wore a wig,
> What could we say?
> Treat him as a gentleman,
> And say 'Good day.'

(PP 134, ll. 1–4)

'If a pig wore a wig' exploits absurd images created by linguistic proximity in order to teach appropriate action and conduct. As in other nonsense texts, the importance of etiquette is clear even in absurd situations. What is interesting, however, is that Rossetti does not write, 'What *would* we say?' but 'What *could* we say', thus suggesting not that there is a stable, given, pre-existing response, but rather that in the *absence* of rules we could respond only according to known structures. These are at once appropriate and inappropriate, for it would be both correct and absurd to bid 'Good day' to the pig, depending on whether one perceives wig or pig as signifying more powerfully. The poem thus opens to the play of semantic alternatives by making sense and nonsense simultaneously.[24] It also highlights what Jean-Jacques Lecercle suggests is the 'textual double-bind, or paradox' of nonsense, which is that it 'tells the reader to abide, and not to abide, by the rules of language.'[25]

The *Sing-Song* poems sustain recognition of the need to establish structures and connections between presupposed objects and words, but while the poems instruct and entertain, they also keep alive a crucial mystery in their exposure of the provisional nature of language and the limitations of normative comprehension. 'Who has seen the wind?' (*PP* 136) points out how affect may be independent of visible stimuli while 'How many seconds in a minute?' (*CP* ii. 30) plays with spans of time which increase as the verse proceeds. Hours and days become years and ages, until the final couplet pushes beyond the parameters of human temporal measurements by asking, 'How many ages in time?' (l. 15). This is a question without any adequate answer: the response in the poem is utterly simple yet gently profound: 'No one knows the rhyme' (l. 16). Here Rossetti uses the temporal relationship between rhyme and time (rhyme works because it aurally reproduces a sound from an earlier moment) but turns the relationship into a negative one: we cannot know the rhyme because we do not know the boundaries of time. Because we are still in language, however, which depends upon and is constructed within a human system governed by our own structuring of time, the rhyme of 'time' and 'rhyme' still persists, despite the negative rejoinder that no one knows it.

COMING IN TIME

Even in apparently simple writings for children, then, Rossetti's interest in mystery, in time, and in what lies beyond human frames of reference emerges clearly. Understandably, however, it is in texts marketed for adults that Rossetti's most extensive explorations of such issues take place. I want to return to 'The Prince's Progress', to look at the ways in which that poem's representations of time overlap with its critique of heroic masculinity. I mentioned earlier that the text undermines the conventions of the masculine quest, but it is not simply in the poem's plot that such challenges to genre and gender appear.

'The Prince's Progress' is critical of its protagonist, figuring him not as a virile hero, but as an unreliable dilettante. The prince is tardy right from the start and lacking in direction and sense of purpose; he is seduced not long after his journey is begun, when, instead of overcoming temptation he succumbs to his own desires and to the wiles of a milkmaid. This is the first of many occasions on which the prince will misread signs. In this instance, as for Laura in *Goblin Market*, consumption leads to a fall:

> Was it milk now, or was it cream?
> Was she a maid, or an evil dream?
> Her eyes began to glitter and gleam;

(ll. 67–9)

'The Prince's Progress' is highly self-conscious about its various literary precedents and is constantly in dialogue with other Romantic and Victorian texts.[26] Both Keatsian and Tennysonian influences are discernible in the fantasized medievalism of Rossetti's poem: the Prince is reminiscent of both Tennyson's Ulysses and his Tristram in 'The Holy Grail', while the transformation of the milkmaid into a witch-like figure and the Prince's succumbing to fleshly temptation recall Keats's 'La Belle Dame Sans Merci' and 'Lamia' – the milkmaid even twists her hair into 'shining serpent-coils' (l. 94) like Keats's snake-woman. Rossetti's use of symbolism and typology connect her poem to Pre-Raphaelite aesthetic practices and creeds as well as to the Tractarian poetics advocated by John Keble, John Henry Newman, and Isaac Williams. The landscape traversed by the Prince strongly recalls that of Robert Browning's 'Childe Roland to the Dark Tower Came' (a poem that also clearly inspires the desolate landscape of Rossetti's 'Cobwebs' (*PP* 43)). The negative formulations Rossetti favours to evoke dreamscapes appear in 'The Prince's Progress' when the land is described as 'lifeless', 'loveless' (l. 133),

> A land of neither life nor death,
> Where no man buildeth or fashioneth,
> Where none draws living or dying breath;
> No man cometh or goeth there,
> No man doeth, seeketh, saith,
> In the stagnant air.

(ll. 139–44)

Despite the static, null environment, the Prince must progress onwards. But while this suggests a linear attitude towards time, the text and Prince both resist this – he with his vicissitudes and the poetry in its repetitions, circumlocutions, and its uncharacteristic lack of linguistic economy. Rossetti reflected in 1888 that, 'Perhaps the nearest approach to a "method" I can lay claim to was a distinct aim at conciseness' (TR 179). 'The Prince's Progress' is, however, one of Rossetti's longest poems, and its spinning in time, its scrambling of temporal terms, and its verbal dallying are part of its point:

> Slip past, slip fast,
> Uncounted hours from first to last,
> Many hours till the last is past,
>   Many hours dwindling to one –
> One hour whose die is cast,
>   One last hour gone.
>
> Come, gone – gone for ever –
> Gone as an unreturning river –
> Gone as to death the merriest liver –
>   Gone as the year at the dying fall –
> Tomorrow, today, yesterday, never –
>   Gone once for all.

(ll. 361–72)

Time passes – at this point in the narrative the Prince has almost drowned and is convalescing – but time also collapses, dissolves, disappears. The poem plays with time and timelessness from its beginning: its first word is a temporal term, 'Till', while the first two stanzas are preoccupied with time passing and with alternative temporalities. The Princess's attendants advise her to 'Sleep, dream and sleep' (l. 10) – that is to enter a different order of time or an atemporal space – for she exists in a kind of stasis in which tomorrow, today, and yesterday are all identical. At the same time, it is one moment that is yearned for: that of the Prince's arrival. But he does not come in time.

Whilst it is clear that the narrative form demands that the Prince ought to fulfil his task, the text seems to take pleasure in resisting literary conventions founded upon heroic action. There is a marked tension between the moral and spiritual requirement that the Prince complete his quest and the impulses of the poetic language, the rhythm and flow of which force the Prince to occupy the kind of liminal state that is ordinarily the province of Rossetti's dreamy women. The Prince's deviations from the linear track and time associated with heroic masculinity destabilize him, and he not only experiences confusion but is almost overwhelmed by elemental properties conventionally associated with the feminine. His desire for a 'second maiden' (l. 298) to bring him some relief summons a rush of 'Waters here, waters there' (l. 306):

> High above, and deep below,
> Bursting, bubbling, swelling the flow,
> Like hill-torrents after the snow, –
>   Bubbling, gurgling, in whirling strife,
> Swaying, sweeping, to and fro, –
>   He must swim for his life.
>
> Which way? – which way? – his eyes grew dim
> With the dizzying whirl – which way to swim?

(ll. 307–14)

Instead of granting the Prince mastery over a maiden, the text floods him and makes him entirely dependent on others to come to his rescue. Thus the Prince is feminized, forced to occupy a psychological space akin to that of his passive Princess, rendering the two less opposed in their subjectivities than their genders would ordinarily suggest.

Throughout the poem, women are seen to have more power and authority than the Prince, whether this power be manifested as pure or corrupt. As Rossetti declares in *The Face of the Deep*, 'Woman is a mighty power for good or for evil' (*FD* 358), and 'The Prince's Progress' illustrates both possibilities. Against the dangerous, seductive temptress milkmaid, Rossetti positions the Princess's loyal attendants, who in the end chide the Prince for his failure to arrive in time. 'You should have wept her yesterday' (l. 531), they declare, 'Her heart was starving all this while | You made it wait' (ll. 489–90). At the end of the poem, the Prince is deprived of any final word, having been silenced by a chorus of disapproving women. As if in revenge for his procrastination, not only does he lose his object of desire, his sleeping beauty, but he loses language too; thus again he is emasculated, prevented from assuming the authoritative identity which his gender and class position would ordinarily guarantee.

This reading of 'The Prince's Progress' is a secular one, but it is important, also, to take account of the poem's Christian symbolism, for the Prince may be read as a figure for sinful man, distracted from the true spiritual path by false charms and attractions, like the male speaker in 'Amor Mundi' (*PP* 99), who fails to act on the warnings he receives and ends up unable to retrace his steps and avoid 'hell's own track' (l. 18). While a Christian allegorical frame is clearly operating in 'The Prince's Progress', however, the poem's dreamy instability and indeterminacy are at least as influential as its specific allegorical dimension.

AFTER DEATH

'The Prince's Progress' speaks from a kind of dream-state outside ordinary temporal frames in order to critique conventions. A similar technique is used in poems that speak from the other side of death. In such poems, speakers are able to look back and contemplate their culture from the 'safety' of a supernatural subjectivity. In the process, social critiques often emerge – Rossetti speaks not only from the other side, but from the side of the 'other'. 'After Death' (*PP* 22), written in 1849, is marked by disruptive power play and cultural commentary, as it takes issue with a typical nineteenth-century artistic representation – that of the beautiful dead woman – and transforms the way such a figure may signify. What Rossetti does with this trope is to turn the silent dead girl into the speaker and then to put her in the privileged position of watching a man's behaviour, unbeknown to him. The man leans above the speaker, utters the lament, 'Poor child, poor child' (l. 7), then turns away in silence 'and I knew he wept' (l. 8). Rossetti subsequently evokes, but writes against, the conventional erotic dynamics of the Victorian deathbed scene, emphasizing that the man does not touch the speaker, take her hand, or touch her shroud. The sonnet then ends:

> He did not love me living; but once dead
> He pitied me; and very sweet it is
> To know he still is warm tho' I am cold.

(ll. 1. 12–14)

25

The spatial and physical autonomy of the speaker seems essential for her articulation and assertion of representational power over the unnamed older man, whose emotional response is summoned only by her demise. From her deathbed, the speaker disrupts conventional masculine/feminine, reason/feeling oppositions, making woman cold and man warm. She also inverts public/private distinctions, so crucial to Victorian bourgeois culture's sense of its own organization, turning the private masculine grief – so private the tears cannot be shown even to a dead girl – into a public affair and thus suggesting that the man's personal response is part of a much larger cultural and gendered behaviour pattern regulated by notions of legitimacy. As voyeurs, readers see into a secret world of masculine emotional vulnerability.

But what precisely are we to make of the adjective 'sweet' in the penultimate line and its relation to the sentiment that follows? It seems not to be meant ironically, nor does it seem adequate to interpret it as a simple statement of masochistic pleasure at the thought that life goes on without her. The speaker seems especially pleased to 'know' that the man is warm, suggesting perhaps that her privileged position as uncanny spectator generates a comforting epistemological certainty, but if this is so she does not, as it were, 'go anywhere' with her knowledge, but rather silences herself, preserving mystery in the very moment that she reveals her own other-worldly perceptions. She seems quite satisfied as she moves into the silence, but as readers we are left pondering, puzzling over what this speaker from beyond could possibly mean.[27]

Where 'After Death' concerns itself with the relation between a young woman and a man, in 'At Home' (PP 64) the 'dead' speaker is a spirit who is looking back at her adult friends as they continue their relatively carefree lives. What she finds is that her friends focus solely on present and future pleasures, 'While no one spoke of yesterday' (l. 20). The speaker invokes the possibility of exerting some ghostly influence over her tunnel-visioned peers, but seems to resist it and accept her displacement and precariousness: on the one hand she is 'of yesterday' (l. 24), but on the other she exists in the present of the poem's articulation. Linda Ruth Williams points out that 'At Home' depicts an uncanny scenario, in which 'Home' is defamiliarized at the same time that it is recognizably familiar to the speaker.[28] The poem plays with projections into the future as well as perspectives on the past, for the speaker's friends look forward to a future 'strong with hope' (l. 17) that 'Tomorrow shall be like | Today, but much more sweet' (ll. 15–16), unconscious that what they look forward to is quite different from 'Today', for it is the place that the speaker actually inhabits. As in 'The Prince's Progress', temporal perspectives are confusingly mixed in order to call into question blinkered patterns of behaviour and to encourage a more far-reaching, long-term vision.

Rossetti's figuring of speakers who hover between life and death or who speak from a posthumous place has been the cause of argument among critics. It has been attributed by Jerome McGann to an interest on Rossetti's part in the doctrine of psychopanny or 'Soul Sleep', which maintained that there was a period between dying and Judgement Day when the soul slept or existed in limbo.[29] This has also been contested; others see Rossetti more entranced by 'entombment...a disturbing sleeplessness of the mind' than by death as 'Soul Sleep'.[30] Whether Rossetti was specifically invoking psychopanny or not, her location of speakers in ambivalent sites does link her work to that of other Victorian women poets, not least Emily Dickinson and Emily Brontë, who also position speakers in liminal or atemporal spaces in order to offer critiques of the dominant paradigms and representational limitations of their cultures. In each case, it seems that reclaiming the body of the dead woman, making her speak instead of allowing her to remain a silent, passive object, is a key motivation and one that represents a significant cultural intervention. It is as if the marginalization experienced by these writers *vis-à-vis* mainstream literary culture was crafted into an aesthetic strategy that exaggerated the culturally circumscribed experience, to radical effect.

Extremity is also a notable feature of certain Rossetti poems that, like some of Dickinson's and Brontë's, feature powerful masculine figures. The last poem I want to discuss in this chapter is 'A Nightmare' (*PP* 57), for this text not only unites concerns with secrets, dreams and sexuality, but also introduces disturbing, threatening energies which will resurface in texts discussed in the next chapter. 'A Nightmare' is a poem that will always keep some of its secrets, for Rossetti tore pages of it from her manuscript notebook, thus ensuring that her fantasies would remain private and safe from any 'too curious' readers. Nevertheless, the remainder of the text is secretive and mysterious as well as dark and troubled – the nightmare is far from the 'delicious fantasy' of 'My Dream'.

The poem conjures its gothic atmosphere in the first two stanzas from a combination of violent and horrific images reminiscent of the opening lines of Tennyson's *Maud*: 'Blood-red seaweeds drip' along Rossetti's coastland (1. 3) and 'In every creek there slopes a dead man's islet' (1. 5).[31] The text also exploits negative formulations such as those found in 'The Prince's Progress' and 'Cobwebs'. It is 'neither night nor day' (1. 8) in this land and all is 'Unripe' (ll. 9, 11), 'unended' (1. 7), and 'unprofitable' (1. 12). There are 'none' to reap the harvest and 'none' to tend the vineyard (ll. 9, 11). 'Living flocks and herds are nowhere found there; | Only ghosts in flocks and shoals' (ll. 13–14). Thus is the place defined by its lacks and absences. We know that it is coastal and that it is a 'watery misty place' (1. 10) where 'Indistinguished hazy ghosts' (1. 15) and 'Troops, yea swarms, of dead men's souls' exist (1. 18). We know also that the speaker has 'a love in ghostland' (1. 1) (changed in a later version of the poem to the more innocuous 'friend'). The sexually charged relationship between the speaker and this masculine figure recalls that found in Emily Brontë's 1837 poem, 'I'll come when thou art saddest',[32] but in Rossetti's case the speaker is not the aggressor, rather she is the victim:

> All night long I feel his presence hover
> Thro' the darkness black as ink.
>
> Without a voice he tells me
> The wordless secrets of death's deep:
> If I sleep, his trumpet voice compels me
> To stalk forth in my sleep:
> If I wake, he rides me like a nightmare;
> I feel my hair stand up, my body creep:
> Without light I see a blasting sight there,
> See a secret I must keep.

(ll. 31–40).

In the later version of the poem, 'rides me' is changed to the less sexually explicit 'hunts me', suggesting that Rossetti was well aware of the erotic connotations of her original verb. Her later substitution notwithstanding, the poem is full of dark sexual energy, quite unlike the flowery meadows of 'What?', the comic orality of 'My Dream', and even the grotesque energies of *Goblin Market*. This is a poem that seems closely related in content to the disturbing dreams Rossetti attributes to Lucy Charlmont in the short story, 'Commonplace' (*PP* 354):

> By day she could forbid her thoughts to shape themselves, even mentally, into words...But by night, when sleep paralysed self-restraint, then her dreams were haunted by distorted spectres of the past...sometimes monstrous, and always impossible to escape from. (*PP* 372)

After such dreams, Lucy awakes, 'struggling and sobbing' (*PP* 372), but tells no one of her fearful nights. 'A Nightmare' is also structured around a secret – 'a secret I must keep'. The visceral references in the final stanza together with the erotic charge of the relation between speaker and ghostly lover (a relation echoed in other texts such as 'The Hour and the Ghost' (*PP* 48) and 'The Poor Ghost' (*CP* i. 120)), suggest that the secret is sexual and unspeakable. The evocation of environment through negative constructions extends to the unutterable content at the poem's core. Without a voice he speaks wordless secrets to her, about mysterious things. She comprehends them as she apprehends him, knowing she must remain both silent and subservient in the face of this 'blasting sight' – an apocalyptic image as well as, perhaps, a fiercely divine one.

The text to some extent betrays the secret by speaking of it at all. The dynamic we observed in *Maude*, of hiding and exposing, is also evident here, though in a more worrying manifestation. 'A Nightmare' simultaneously dare not let itself be read and begs for release from the haunted psychic landscape it inhabits. It cannot speak what it has prohibited itself, but it exposes the energy that leads to the prohibition. A troubled, troubling dynamic is figured and this is related to an encounter with a threatening masculinity. It is interesting that Rossetti chose never to publish the poem, but that she did circulate it, some years after its composition, among members of the Portfolio Society, a women's literary network active in the 1860s that included Barbara Leigh Smith (Bodichon), Bessie Parkes, and

Adelaide Procter.[33] So Rossetti deemed the poem readable (with some manuscript changes), by fellow women artists, but did not consider it suitable for public consumption. Again, the poet's self-protective instincts come to the fore, and her decision to suppress the poem suggests she was well aware of the fantasies it suggests and the shocking effect these might have on mid-Victorian readers. Nevertheless, throughout the 1850s Rossetti was composing works that explore many of the same issues as does 'A Nightmare'. Her investigations of feminine identity, masculine–feminine relations, and, specifically, the problems associated with regulating, releasing, and representing the energies of the female body are crucially important in the history of Victorian women's writing. It is these sensual, sexual–textual investigations that will provide the focus for Chapter 2.

2

Body

Three sang of love together: one with lips
    Crimson, with cheeks and bosom in a glow,
Flushed to the yellow hair and finger tips;
    And one there sang who soft and smooth as snow
    Bloomed like a tinted hyacinth at a show;
And one was blue with famine after love,
    Who like a harpstring snapped rang harsh and low
The burden of what those were singing of.
One shamed herself in love; one temperately
    Grew gross in soulless love, a sluggish wife;
One famished died for love. Thus two of three
    Took death for love and won him after strife;
One droned in sweetness like a fattened bee:
    All on the threshold, yet all short of life.

('A Triad' (*PP* 50, ll. 1–14))

'A Triad', written in 1856, is one of Rossetti's typically cutting and uncompromising representations of the amatory possibilities available to Victorian women. The love that women are socially encouraged to pursue brings shame, despair, and death; even the supposedly 'successful' wife survives like a prize pig, in a most unenviable state of complacency and lifelessness. To shame oneself as a mistress, to shrivel away in 'famished' spinsterhood, or to be bound to a 'soulless' marriage: Rossetti paints woeful destinies for one and all.

Acute social criticism exists in Rossetti's work in tandem with her emphasis on dreams, secrets, and the vanity of earthly preoccupations. There is a marked tension between her resistance to dominant bourgeois ideologies and her longing to retreat from the world: explicit protests against the injustices and inequalities of mid-Victorian England are paralleled by imaginative recourse to a utopian afterlife or, as in 'From the

Antique' (*PP* 37), to a fantasy that one could simply cease to be:

> It's a weary life, it is; she said: –
> Doubly blank in a woman's lot:
> I wish and I wish I were a man;
> Or, better than any being, were not:

(ll. 1–4)

The opening lines here are proto-feminist in their expression of dissatisfaction, but the desire to claim the privileges of masculinity is soon overpowered by the wish to be 'nothing at all in all the world, | Not a body and not a soul' (ll. 5–6). Existence is so weary and leaves women so 'short of life' that death seems a welcome release – an extreme stance, but one that in its extremity signals the depths of feminine frustration.

CULTURAL CRITIC

Rossetti may be criticized for the escapism of poems such as 'From the Antique'; certainly she does not offer political solutions to social injustice. Nevertheless, her treatment of a whole range of nineteenth-century ideologies marks her out as a passionate and singular critic of bourgeois culture: Victorian capitalism, materialism, consumerism, and commodity culture are reviled, social inequality is depicted as sinful, the poor and oppressed are vociferously defended, and those who cannot speak publicly are spoken for. To the end of her life she continued to express her abhorrence of injustice: 'The contrast between London luxury and London destitution is really appalling,' she wrote to Ellen Proctor; 'all sorts of gaities advertised, and deaths by exposure or starvation recorded, in the same newspaper'.[1] Rossetti was also a fierce defender of animal rights and campaigned vigorously against vivisection, a practice she perceived as 'cruelty of revolting magnitude', 'horror of horrors' (*FL* 51). Her concern for the underprivileged is felt particularly in respect of women, especially factory girls, minors, and the sexually abused; Rossetti supported many of the campaigns that attracted feminists in the late nineteenth century and wrote scores of poems and stories that reveal profound resistance to patriarchal values and sexual double standards.

It might seem surprising, then, that Rossetti refused to align herself with nineteenth-century feminists' demands for access to higher education or women's suffrage. While many of her activist acquaintances and fellow women poets supported the franchise bills, Rossetti took exception to the proposed legislation and, in correspondence with Augusta Webster in the late 1870s, she explains why this is so. Her well-known comments on the issue are both extraordinary and typical of Rossetti's highly individual perspective: she twists and skews normative ideologies, oscillating between fundamentally conservative and remarkable radical stances.

On the conservative front, she opposes the bill on account of an orthodox Christian belief that an 'unalterable distinction' exists between men and women and their 'position, duties, privileges' (*PP* 418). She does not believe that the 'present social movement tends on the whole to uphold Xtianity',[2] and, since she earnestly desires to 'attain to the character of a humble orthodox Christian' (*PP* 418), she 'cannot aim at "women's rights" '.[3] At the same time, she finds the exclusion of married women from the suffrage unacceptable, asking who better to 'protect the interests of themselves and of their offspring?': 'I do think if anything ever does sweep away the barrier of sex, and make the female not a giantess or a heroine but at once and full grown into a hero and a giant, it is that mighty maternal love which makes little birds and little beasts as well as little women matches for very big adversaries' (*PP* 418–19).[4]

Reflecting upon the special power of maternal love and making use of the cultural importance ascribed to the Victorian mother, Rossetti imagines beyond the strictures of oppositional sexual difference and the gendered language of terms such as 'giantess' (acknowledging that such terms, including, perhaps, 'poetess', deprive the bearer of the status of mature, 'full grown' adult). Much more radically and totally unpredictably, she also states that, 'if female rights are sure to be overborne for lack of female voting influence, then I confess I feel disposed to shoot ahead of my instructresses, and to assert that female *M.P.*'s are only right and reasonable' (*PP* 418). Rossetti's perspective in this final comment may seem right and reasonable in a present-day context, but few of her contemporaries articulated such a far-reaching vision and it is only in the late 1990s that British

33

women M.P.'s number more than a tiny fraction of the parliamentary cohort.

Rossetti is intriguingly unclear and contradictory both about what constitute women's rights and how best to remedy gender-based injustice, but throughout her work she is unrelenting in her exposure of female suffering and resilience. Her concern about male power over women emerges in *The Face of the Deep*, in which she claims that women are more likely to 'undergo than to inflict hurt, to be cut...than to cut' (*FD* 410). This is a perspective that runs through her earliest poems of betrayal and abandonment. To some extent such criticism of errant masculine behaviour is not unusual in nineteenth-century women's writing: Rossetti inherited a tradition of women's poetry, shaped particularly by the work of Felicia Hemans and Letitia Landon, in which faithless men were depicted as the norm.[5] However that may be, Rossetti's exposure of unjust male–female interrelations is especially stark: the perspective that '"Young men aye were fickle found | Since summer trees were leafy"' (*CP* iii. 143) runs through a host of early poems including 'Heart's Chill Between', 'Undine', 'Ariadne to Theseus', and 'Fair Margaret', among others (*PP* 13, 15; *CP* iii. 121, 84).

'Cousin Kate' (*PP* 70) is a typically intense tale of a 'cottage maiden' (l. 1) lured by a lord 'To lead a shameless shameful life' (l. 11):

> He wore me like a silken knot,
>   He changed me like a glove;
> So now I moan, an unclean thing,
>   Who might have been a dove.

(ll. 13–16)

Like Maggie Crowe in the short story 'Vanna's Twins' (*PP* 314), the speaker of 'Cousin Kate' has been left with inadequate means to care for her child – irresponsible fatherhood being another of Rossetti's favourite targets.

Dante Gabriel Rossetti, who both supported his sister in getting her work published and often succeeded in exerting artistic influence over her output, sometimes took exception to Christina's social critique. 'The Iniquity of the Fathers Upon the Children' (*PP* 200) was a source of sibling disagreement: this tale of an illegitimate child was defended by Christina on the grounds that it is a dramatic monologue and that as a poet she has every right to represent others' experience, however 'unpleasant' such experience may be. She also emphasizes that her representation of the wider social problem of illegitimacy is cast in a personal context: 'the field is occupied by a single female figure whose internal portrait is set forth in her own words' (*LCR* i. 234, Letter 258). In stressing thus the personal tone of the piece, Christina manœuvres her brother into a final acceptance of the manuscript,[6] but the poem itself makes clear that the personal and socio-political cannot be separated: subjective experience is socially conditioned and discourses of gender, religion, class, and national identity all affect Rossetti's portrayal of the illegitimate girl's life.

Rossetti gravitates towards writing in the first person, or narrating the stories of two or three women, for what interests her are the emotional and physical consequences of feminine subordination as much as its wider causes. Although her poems rarely include overt political comment, their radicalism consists in their treatment of female desire. Rossetti is unusually daring in her exposure of the difficulties of managing female passion – difficulties frequently depicted through representations of the body that betray turmoil within. The sexually active woman of 'A Triad' is, like Laura in *Goblin Market*, defined by her aroused body; her lips, cheeks, bosom, and finger tips flush and glow with desire and thus she is seen immediately to be at risk. Surging physical sensations and emotional frustration launch many of Rossetti's tales of femininity, and, though in many texts she tries to find a way to calm and soothe her fervently passionate women, she ordinarily fails to find any permanent method of sedation. So the textual process begins again, its spokespersons unappeased.

Some of Rossetti's most important work represents the changes and crises that occur in the minds and bodies of young women as they negotiate the difficult passage to maturity. Rossetti's own adolescence was deeply traumatic, marked by illness, depression, self-hatred, and religious obsession. She had barely emerged from this painful period when she became engaged to the painter James Collinson – a union that was to culminate in acute disappointment for Rossetti when the relationship ended in 1850.[7] Some of the poet's personal suffering finds its way into her work, in anguished lyrics such as 'She sat and sang alway', 'An End', 'Oh roses for the flush of youth', and 'Shut Out' (*PP* 17, 20, 18, 45). It is important, however, to be wary of ascribing autobiographical experience too rigidly to Rossetti's poems of loss and betrayal, for she wrote of disappointment in love long before any known relationship.

BODILY FANTASIES

Although Rossetti tackles issues of adolescent feminine subjectivity in prose stories, and in lyric and narrative poems, some of her most sustained examinations, as we have seen, occur in texts generically identifiable as fantasy, a literary mode that departs from consensual reality in order to throw into relief and critique the social norms from which it springs.[8] The fairy tale – traditionally a genre in which questions of power, desire, and social mobility are central – inspires both the short story 'Hero' (*PP* 292), and its much better-known sister, *Goblin Market*. In both these texts, girls are transformed from adolescents into wives and mothers, and, as this process of maturation is pursued, the texts engage in startling explorations of issues surrounding feminine agency, the social and economic management of female bodies, and women's relation to money and commodity culture. A brief discussion of the context from which Rossetti's fairy tales emerged assists in understanding how they signify.

'Hero' and *Goblin Market* were written in a decade that produced more literary and artistic representations of fairy worlds than had ever previously appeared. The popularity of fairy stories increased following the translation of the Grimms', Perrault's, and Andersen's tales; Victorian readers responded positively to the characteristic blend of morality and fantasy offered by such texts. By the 1850s there was a veritable fairy 'craze' and stories, paintings, illustrations, and books classifying supernatural beings commanded a sizeable share of the Victorian market place.

Writing in *Household Words* in 1853, Charles Dickens emphasized the national importance of fairy stories in an oppressive 'utilitarian age'. In his defence of their value, however, he attempts to fix the tales: 'To preserve them in their usefulness, they must be as much preserved in their simplicity and purity, as if they were actual facts.'[9] This perspective is flawed on two counts: it not only denies the metamorphic history of fairy tales, which pass from generation to generation, through history and between cultures, but also ignores the possibility of creating new stories, which many Victorian writers were keen to do. Women writers of the time took to the form in great numbers and in the process revised dominant representations of femininity: Jean Ingelow, Mary De Morgan, Juliana Ewing, and Louisa Molesworth, among many others, produced stories featuring independent, resourceful heroines who have great adventures, illicit relations with other transgressive women or who manifest superior intellectual and physical skills.[10] Just as previous generations of female story-tellers had disseminated tales that spoke symbolically of women's lives and predicaments, so Victorian writers continued to reshape fantasy narratives and to challenge the limitations imposed upon women's lives and movements.[11]

Both 'Hero' and *Goblin Market* form a part of this female literary tradition. The two texts are also preoccupied with the commodity culture from which they grew and with the relation of women to what Elizabeth Helsinger identifies as the 'economics of consumption'.[12] Helsinger's reading of *Goblin Market*, together with other 1990s essays that focus on the poem's treatment of material exchange and the market place, emphasize Rossetti's awareness of women's position as both agents and objects in the Victorian political economy.[13] Though relatively neglected, 'Hero' is also interested in the feminine predicament *vis-à-vis* commodity culture and I discuss this story first, since it is in important ways a precursor to *Goblin Market*.

The story itself is simple: Hero, a discontented girl, encounters a supernatural being and is granted her wish to become the supreme object of desire. After a series of metamorphic experiences that are only intermittently desir-able, she realizes that home is where the greatest satisfaction lies, and returns to marry and raise children. 'Hero' shares with *Goblin Market* some aspects of the cautionary tale, but it also targets Victorian middle-class culture very specifically. This cultural specificity can be seen from the beginning of the story, where the narrator tempts the reader to discover the enchanted location wherein her tale is set.

'If you consult the authentic map of Fairyland (recently published by Messrs Moon, Shine, and Co.)...' (*PP* 292). Thus opens 'Hero', instantly connecting fantasy and social reality. This is not the ahistorical world that many fairy stories (including *Goblin Market*) pretend to occupy and that Dickens attempts to preserve, but a time when fairyland is mapped, charted, published, and subject to ownership and copyright laws. The mid-century expansion in the publishing industry and the commodification of fairy tales themselves provide the context for Rossetti's satirical opening sentence. The publication of maps demarcating 'other' lands also suggests the colonial consolidation taking place in the mid-century, while Rossetti's insistence on the importance of authenticity satirizes the Victorian cultural preoccupation with proving the existence of supernatural beings and locating them 'authentically' according to geography and history, as well as ontology.[14]

As Rossetti's opening sentence suggests, wherever fairies live they do not escape the operations of capitalism and imperialism. Fairy lands are mapped and charted, while fairy products, the diamonds and opals of 'Elf-side', are gathered and traded by the community of 'semi-barbarous fishermen' who live across the water to the west (*PP* 292). The representation of the fishermen erases distinctions between colonized and colonizer: on the one hand, the men are depicted as uncivilized, but on the other, their barbarity is manifested in economic practices typical of mid-Victorian culture. Exploitative child labour is an integral part of the fisherman's economy, as is the routine stripping of the material wealth of the fairy 'colony' (*PP* 304). Thus is it made abundantly clear that, while the tale is set in a fantasized space, it is also inextricably connected to the culture and historical moment from which it emanates and to which it speaks.

A direct critique of materialistic values occurs in the tale, following Hero's metamorphosis into a diamond (probably modelled on the Koh-i-noor diamond exhibited at the Great Exhibition of 1851). As the diamond, Hero is fought over by the fishermen until the physically strongest claims the prize as his own. Rampant materialism brings communal strife, just as it does in another of Rossetti's stories, 'A Safe Investment' (included in the *Commonplace* collection of 1870). Hero's own investment in materialism is evident in her enjoyment of objectification; she likes being placed on velvet, encased in glass, and bid for, she is happy to be a commodity that fetches millions, thrilled to be an object that can be bought and sold.

The relationship between monetary value, national product, and desire is exposed throughout 'Hero'. Although the objects into which the heroine is transformed vary between animal, vegetable, and mineral, all are united by their commercial and cultural worth. The Koh-i-noor diamond, due to be set into the Crown Jewels, signifies both the wealth of the domestic Royal Family and the Empire that sustains such wealth. The heart of Princess Lily and the voice of the opera singer, Melice Rapta, indicate the high value placed on celebrity bodies who function as repositories for the fantasies of the nation. Even the rare plant cultivated by Uncle Treeh, grown from a seedling exported from the fairy colony, exposes the way in which the Victorian obsession with botany is connected to the wider commodification of the natural world brought about through imperialist commerce.

During her metamorphic journey, Hero circulates and is subject to exchange, like a currency. Like money, she is not valuable in herself, but her presence signifies the value of that to which she is bound, much as beautiful women can signify the wealth and power of older, less beautiful men. Her desire to be the supreme 'object' (PP 295) of admiration renders her unable to escape associated conditions of powerlessness: throughout her journey she is governed by arbitrary events, functioning as an allegory of the feminine subject-as-victim: passed around, fulfilling fantasies, ultimately dispensable.

Hero is saved the conventional feminine fate only because, throughout her metamorphic journey, she has no body. She is protected, unlike other girls who venture into the market place and its world of sexual exchange, since her material body is absent, 'at rest, and crowned with lilies' (PP 297). Rossetti circumvents the problematic material reality of the female body and the cultural regulations surrounding its movements and expression by splitting flesh and spirit. This opens the way for Hero to have experiences that are morally instructive and fantastically exciting, but do not prohibit the possibility of final redemption. As in *Goblin Market*, where Laura is allowed to survive her transgression rather than end up dead, Rossetti conceives a strategy by which Hero will be able, in one sense at least, to have her cake and eat it too. She fulfils a set of fantasies that were unrealizable in the ordinary lives of Victorian girls, experiencing fame, fortune, glory, and travel, but (technically) she does not compromise her virginity and suitability for the marriage market.

Hero's encounter with Princess Fay occurs when she is 15 years of age, following a familial misunderstanding that leaves her 'Stung by supposed indifference' (PP 294). She exhibits the classic fairy-tale feminine sins of pride, jealousy, and vanity, but her dissatisfaction, self-consciousness, and sensitivity are all attributable to the changes brought about by puberty. The motherless child finds no reassurance of her acceptability and normality in the fishermen's culture, but the discovery of Princess Fay, by the water, in a flute-lipped shell propelled by a fish, is an encounter that brings the girl face to face with a supernatural sexual symbol.

The Fairy Queen and her people are considerably more sensitive to Hero's predicament than are the fishermen. It is imperative, they realize, to protect her virginal body, to safeguard her against her own narcissistic yearning that lays her wide open to the whims or obsessions of masculine fantasy. The fairies are bound by their own statutes to grant Hero her wish, but the Fairy Queen warns her of the possible consequences of her desire:

> In you every man shall find his taste satisfied. In you one shall recognise his ideal of loveliness, another shall bow before the impersonation of dignity. One shall be thrilled by your voice, another fascinated by your wit and inimitable grace. He who prefers colour shall dwell upon your complexion, hair, eyes; he who worships intellect shall find in you his superior; he who is ambitious shall feel you to be a prize more august than an empire. I cannot ennoble the taste of those who look upon you: I can but cause that in you all desire shall be gratified. If sometimes you chafe under a trivial homage, if sometimes you are admired rather for what you have than for what you are, accuse your votaries, – accuse, if you will, yourself, but accuse not me. (PP 296–7)

As it turns out, the Fairy Queen's fears regarding sexual exploitation are not realized in the tale. The closest Hero comes to direct sexual encounter is when she metamorphoses into the heart of Princess Lily and spends several days secluded with the new

Prince in a palace full of a hundred mirrors. Here she enjoys an astonishing erotic experience as she is 'worshipped' by the Prince 'at dawn, or lazy noon, or mysterious twilight – for indeed the process went on every day and all day' (*PP* 298–9). What is more, Hero gets away with this because her body is not implicated in the sexual encounter. After moving on from Princess Lily and eventually tiring of her constant metamorphoses, she is allowed to return home, is accepted back into her community, and 'wooed and won' by her fisherman lover (*PP* 304).

Hero's journey enables her to leave the paternal home and gives her temporary escape from the fixture of her subject position and the predictability of her future with Forss (who, though apparently kind, has an alarmingly authoritative name). It gives her a chance to learn her own lessons and allows her a degree of independence impossible in the domestic context: instead of becoming an object of exchange between father and fiancé, acceding to Forss's desire to have Hero's body in (or as) a 'tight house of his own' (*PP* 294), she has an incredible adventure. True to a long history of metamorphic narratives, she discovers in the process a new and more mature identity through splitting away from her ordinary corporeality.[15]

In Hero's passionate longing for her old life to return and her subsequent embrace of the role of wife and mother normative ideologies resurface, but though Hero becomes an advocate for the view that home is safest and best, she also becomes a storyteller. Like Laura in *Goblin Market*, the woman who has adventured and transgressed becomes the disseminator of new myths, enchanting her children with tales of her early days. As Hero stirs the transformative power of her children's imaginations, she lodges extraordinary possibility in their minds – which in turn affects their bodies as eyes kindle, cheeks flush, and breath quickens (*PP* 304). Although Hero's assurances that home is better than Fairyland and true love superior to preeminence come with a 'convincing smile' (*PP* 304), the effect of telling the story at all is to estrange her listeners to everyday expectations.[16] The limitations of constituting oneself as the object of another's desire are highlighted, but so is the importance of discovering one's own authentic desire; thus feminine education is also, in this instance, partially feminist.

COME BUY

Goblin Market, like 'Hero', shows young women's desire for adventure and the dangers that accompany such longing, but, where 'Hero' circumvents the problem of the body, *Goblin Market* tackles it head on. Adolescent bodies are again the focus of attention and on several occasions Laura's form is seen to change, to go beyond its ordinary confines, to extend or attenuate, to lose or gain weight. Typical pubescent changes are exaggerated until they become grotesque: the bodies of both girls and goblins are in flux, and so is the language of the poem, for throughout *Goblin Market* there is a close connection between the motility of form and word. Bodies and language are unstable and provocative: the text demonstrates the power of seduction in the sensuality of its opening lines, which whet the reader's appetite and activate the mouths and tongues of any who read it aloud:

> Apples and quinces,
> Lemons and oranges,
> Plump unpecked cherries,
> Melons and raspberries,
> Bloom-down-cheeked peaches,
> Swart-headed mulberries,
> Wild free-born cranberries,
> Crab-apples, dewberries,
> Pine-apples, blackberries,
> Apricots, strawberries; –
>
> .   .   .   .   .
>
> Taste them and try:

(ll. 5–14, 25)

Laura and Lizzie are aroused, for, despite their 'cautioning lips', they have 'tingling cheeks and finger-tips' (ll. 38–9). Blushes often symbolize erotic response in Victorian literature, as lower-body arousal is displaced to the face, and here, as in 'A Triad' and 'Hero', the increased blood-flow to sensitive zones of the body acts in blatant defiance of propriety. The conflict between transgressive desire and moral injunction is made clear in Laura's reaction:

'Lie close,' Laura said,
Pricking up her golden head:
'We must not look at goblin men,
We must not buy their fruits:'

(ll. 40–3)

Laura's physical movement is proleptic: her pricked-up head anticipates her fall, whereas Lizzie protects herself by shutting off or plugging her body: 'She thrust a dimpled finger | In each ear, shut eyes and ran' (ll. 67–8). Laura is fascinated by the 'whisk-tailed', 'cat-faced', 'rat-paced' goblin merchants (ll. 106, 109, 110), and impulsively she speaks, opening her mouth instead of remaining silent and sealed, as good girls should. Laura cannot control her body or her language – the 'dripping' pitcher she carries (l. 263) signifies her lack of physical containment, while her linguistic indulgence is marked in her production of poetic images: 'all my gold is on the furze | That shakes in windy weather | Above the rusty heather' (ll. 120–2). Her voracious feasting on the goblin 'fruit globes' (l. 128) occurs as she gives in to her longing:

She sucked and sucked and sucked the more
Fruits which that unknown orchard bore;
She sucked until her lips were sore;

(ll. 134–6)

This frenzied consumption far exceeds the Edenic model it draws upon, as one bite of an apple is rewritten as uncontrollable orality. In Rossetti's work feasting always suggests a problematical lack of self-control, exhibited for instance by the hideous children of *Speaking Likenesses*, whose 'stuffing without limit' is a marker of their immorality (*PP* 335), or in the frozen figures of 'The Dead City' (*PP* 138), whose petrification occurs following their consumption of a sumptuous banquet.

Laura's gorging makes her vulnerable: Victorian readers would have understood the physical and spiritual defilement implied in her succumbing to the goblins' temptation, and in most Victorian literature such illicit sensual indulgence would lead inexorably to death. Even in texts that attempt to treat fallen women sympathetically, such as Elizabeth Gaskell's *Ruth* (1853), the erring woman eventually dies as punishment for her sins. But Laura, like Hero, gets away with it, not because she escapes her body but because Lizzie braves an encounter with the goblins, enacting a full-grown heroic sacrifice for her sister and proving that a little woman can be a match for furious adversaries. Lizzie's heroism and Christ-like self-sacrifice is predicated, however, on her willingness to break away from feminine propriety. Like the Princess in 'A Royal Princess' (*PP* 176), who defies authority and puts herself in danger for a cause she feels to be right and just (Rossetti's princess bears a striking resemblance to Princess Diana), Lizzie must defy the conservatism with which she has been identified and to which she feels allegiance.

The scene in which Lizzie procures the fruit to save Laura is violent and vicious:

> They trod and hustled her,
> Elbowed and jostled her,
> Clawed with their nails,
> Barking, mewing, hissing, mocking,
> Tore her gown and soiled her stocking,
> Twitched her hair out by the roots,
> Stamped upon her tender feet,
> Held her hands and squeezed their fruits
> Against her mouth to make her eat.

(ll. 400–7)

When extracts from *Goblin Market* were printed in *Playboy* in 1973, this was one of the scenes depicted – an attempted rape presented as erotic stimulation for men.[17] This is a useful reminder that the poem can be and has been consumed in many ways – readers gorge upon it, but the poem also resists this, just as Lizzie resists physical and linguistic indulgence: 'Lizzie uttered not a word; | Would not open lip from lip | Lest they should cram a mouthful in' (ll. 430–2). Lizzie's purity of action and motive enables her to secure the antidote to Laura's sickness and offer herself to her sister free of fear and guilt. The encounter that occurs at this point in the poem is one of the most intensely erotic and sensual invitations in canonical Victorian verse:

> Come and kiss me.
> Never mind my bruises,
> Hug me, kiss me, suck my juices
> Squeezed from goblin fruits for you,

> Goblin pulp and goblin dew.
> Eat me, drink me, love me;
> Laura, make much of me:

(ll. 466–72)

Laura's reaction is similarly passionate:

> She clung about her sister,
> Kissed and kissed and kissed her:
>
> . . . .
>
> She kissed and kissed her with a hungry mouth

(ll. 485–6, 492)

Just as surely as the goblins' attack on Lizzie signifies masculine sexual aggression, so this scene represents same-sex, incestuous desire and activity. Although the sexual identity 'lesbian' was not an available discursive category in the mid-Victorian period, Rossetti's text so displaces or modifies patriarchal and heterosexual paradigms that it contributes significantly to the 'lesbian continuum' – a literary tradition not necessarily based on the sexual practice of authors (which is often extremely difficult if not impossible to establish), but on women writers' compassionate and sensual portrayals of same-sex relations.[18]

It is also important to acknowledge that in this scene from *Goblin Market*, as elsewhere in Rossetti's work, language that has sexuality as its referent also engages directly with Christian texts and contexts, which does not dilute the sex but does complicate the ways it may be understood. The scene between Laura and Lizzie shows the manner in which the flesh, the word, and the Word are bound up in one another, for Lizzie's invitation is clearly cast in biblical rhetoric that evokes the Eucharistic feast. Lizzie's previous enduring of the goblins' assault connects her body and spirit to that of Christ, but here we have a *female* Christ experiencing a physical passion. The overarching narrative of temptation, sacrifice, and redemption differs from conventional Christian allegory, because in *Goblin Market* women are both sinners *and* redeemers, sinned against and redeemed. Female sexuality does not bring about the downfall of the world and Lizzie is not just 'good', she is astoundingly strong.

Goblin Market was composed in 1859, while Rossetti was working at the St Mary Magdalen Penitentiary at Highgate.

45

Here Anglican sisters and volunteers like Rossetti strove to re-educate fallen women through religious and moral instruction and retrain them as domestic servants. In telling Laura's tale, *Goblin Market* supports the institution's emphasis on the potential power of sorority, but it also fundamentally resists the discursive regulations imposed at Highgate, for the women were not allowed to speak of their past experiences or read literature considered inflammatory to the passions, let alone become storytellers themselves. When Laura is reborn and redeemed, however, her narrative is transformed into an orally transmitted myth of sisterhood, presented less as a cautionary tale than as a story of female heroism, replete with pleasures and fears:

> Laura would call the little ones
> And tell them of her early prime,
>
> .   .   .   .
>
> Would talk about the haunted glen,
> The wicked, quaint fruit-merchant men
>
> .   .   .   .   .   .
>
> Would tell them how her sister stood
> In deadly peril to do her good,

(ll. 548–9, 552–3, 557–8)

We never know the effect of Laura's words on her 'little ones', whether her story initiates so as to protect them from temptation or whether they, like their mother (and Hero), will have to discover for themselves the pleasures and pains of feminine transgression. It is a mark of Rossetti's alternative myth-making in her fairy tale that Laura is not silenced any more than she is made to die; the conclusions of both *Goblin Market* and 'Hero' emphasize the need for women to take charge of their own narratives, in defiance of the Penitentiary's code of silence and in support of the wider cultural shift towards women seizing the right to make their stories public.

GOBLIN READING

And what of the goblins themselves? Are they simply assorted lecherous men, prone to the kind of fantastic metamorphoses that also appear in 'Hero' and Rossetti's other fairy tale, 'Nick'

(*PP* 286)?[19] Or is their representation indicative of more specific mid-Victorian anxieties? Fairy stories inevitably reproduce cultural concerns with gender, social class, race, and national identity, and at the point when *Goblin Market* is composed, the Crimean War is not long over, the American Civil War is soon to begin, the 'Woman Question' is generating increasing discursive momentum, and one of the effects of British imperialism is the immigration to England of peoples from many colonized parts of the globe. Fears about working-class uprising, Irish immigration, and racial miscegenation all pertain to the representation of the goblins as animalistic and bestial. Rossetti's 'goblins' may signify a class of itinerant workers, perhaps specifically Irish, considered to be unfit sexual partners for bourgeois girls. Or, as Cora Kaplan has argued, *Goblin Market* may be seen to reproduce and compound Victorian fears about black–white miscegenation,[20] changing our understanding of 'White and golden Lizzie stood' (l. 408) from a description of innocent virginity and Christ-like bearing to an image of white supremacy, anxious to retain its claim to privilege and superiority.

The interrogation of *Goblin Market* in the context of mid-nineteenth-century imperialism is a trend in criticism that is opening up exciting new ways of reading. There will always remain some difficulty, however, in determining what the goblins signify precisely, since instability itself is integral to their representation. Not only are they visibly heterogeneous, but at the level of discourse, too, they represent motility. Their speech veers between the practised, repetitive call of the market place (ll. 4, 31, 104), the cajoling tones of seduction (ll. 77–9), and animalistic and imitative whistling, mewing, hissing, and barking (ll. 112–14, 402).[21] The parodic aspects of goblin discourse reach an extreme in the case of one who 'Cried "Pretty Goblin" still for "Pretty Polly"' (l. 113). Here mimicry doubles and redoubles as goblin imitates bird imitates human speech, scrambling the distinction between authentic and parodic, disrupting the boundaries between human and animal, animal and goblin, goblin and human. The mutating language, like the goblin bodies, challenges ordinary categories, generates a dangerous but exciting sense of lawlessness and excess, and resists interpretative closure.

The poem represents both the appeal of and the cultural

prohibitions against union with 'others', whether that term be defined sexually, socially, racially, religiously, linguistically, or ontologically. The political implications of *Goblin Market* shift when the poem is considered as a cultural intervention that signifies beyond the confines of bourgeois gender debates. Despite its own attempt to evade history, to refuse any temporal frame beyond the 'once upon a time' of the fairy tale, the historical moment of its production has left numerous traces in its textuality. Rossetti may have refused to be drawn on the poem, but generations of readers continue to assess its cultural intervention and to propose new readings of its significance as a cultural document. Like Caroline Norton, we do and must continue to ask, 'What is it?'

FILLING HIS DREAM

The troublesome bodies of *Goblin Market* reappear in much of Rossetti's work, if not in goblin form then in other manifestations of sexuality both external and internal. 'To flee the flesh' ('Tune me, O Lord, into one harmony' (*CP* ii. 255, 1. 9)) is a strong impulse, but by definition not possible this side of death, so Rossetti's women must continually deal with all aspects of their problematical corporeality. Sometimes they are uncomfortably confronted with masculine perceptions; the female body as a site of voyeuristic consumption appears in 'Light Love' (*CP* i. 136), where the betraying male lover boasts about the attractions of his new love to the woman he is about to abandon:

> 'Ripe-blooming she, as thou forlorn.
> Ripe-blooming she, my rose, my peach;
>
> .   .   .   .
> I watch her tremble in my reach;
>   She reddens, my delight;
>   She ripens, reddens in my sight.'

(ll. 45–6, 48–50)

This explicitly erotic description of the new woman's sexual charms is grossly insensitive to the feelings of the 'ex' – an insensitivity that serves to highlight the compulsive drive of a pornographic masculine sexuality. Rossetti is bold here, as she is in her fascinating sonnet 'In an Artist's Studio' (*PP* 52), in which the male artist (almost certainly modelled upon Dante Gabriel) 'feeds' upon the face of his model (l. 9), blinded by his own fantasy to the sad, wan woman who is perceived by the speaker of the poem.[22] There is a sense, in many of Rossetti's tortured ballads and sonnets, of a difference of view that is unbridgeable: the male artist, the male lover, sees woman, 'Not as she is, but as she fills his dream' ('In an Artist's Studio', l. 14), whereas 'We' perceive 'her hidden just behind those screens' (l. 3). The collective pronoun used in 'In an Artist's Studio' is intriguing, for it suggests a community of women able to see through men's representations, who are not taken in by 'his dream' and who resist the way that women, in all their subtleties and differences, become Woman: 'The same one meaning, neither more nor less' (l. 8).

Escape from the world of heterosexual relations is sometimes proposed as a solution to women's problems, but there is only ever temporary respite from sexuality, for in many subtle ways the body always returns. In 'Three Nuns' (*CP* iii. 187), the speaker refers to her earlier experience of being seen by men and judged attractive (ll. 22–3), but even when she escapes into a convent, shaves off her curls, and curtains herself 'from intruding eyes' (l. 30), she cannot escape her own physicality. In longing for the 'flush of Paradise' (l. 32), her rhetoric betrays her, for even the mystical union of souls to come is cast in terms that summon fleshiness. In these cases desire cannot be projected onto men any more than flesh and word can ultimately be divided, despite the effort to figure spaces beyond both. Contrary to the common notion of Rossetti as ascetic, her descriptions of the desired and desirable are characterized by *jouissance*.

SISTERS

A favourite technique of Rossetti's is to split her portrayals of women into different parts so that contrasting perspectives may be debated. Laura and Lizzie are obvious examples; the sisters are both different and similar, typical in their alliterative naming – a device that draws attention to their fictional nature – and in the way they function as ciphers for particular attitudes and ideologies. 'Noble Sisters', 'Sister Maude', 'Maiden-Song', *Maude*, and 'Commonplace' are other texts depicting sororal

49

relations (*PP* 72, 73, 180, 251, 354) and through these relationships they portray not only solidarity but fierce conflicts and competition between women. 'The Lowest Room' (*PP* 150) is, however, one of the most interesting of these 'sister' texts, for it yokes questions of gender and the body to issues of creativity and artistic representation: it is a poem of struggle, not of triumph, but its pain and its suffering are an incontrovertible part of its power.

'The Lowest Room' was written in 1856; biographical evidence suggests that it draws upon (but reworks) the relationship between Rossetti and her intellectually talented but morally and ideologically conservative sister Maria, to whom *Goblin Market* is dedicated. The drama that unfolds in the course of 'The Lowest Room' illustrates the frustration and rage of its energetic female speaker, whose creative and intellectual ambitions are thwarted by a restrictive social order, but it also examines the feelings of inferiority, guilt, and shame that accompany rebellion. Virginia Woolf said of Rossetti, 'Modest as you were, still you were drastic' (*PP* 467): 'The Lowest Room' illustrates both these qualities in abundance.

At the start of the poem, the speaker likens herself to a flower kept away from the light (l. 1), fires desperate questions at her domesticated sister regarding the purpose of existence (ll. 5–8), and struggles with the idea that she must accept secondary status in life (ll. 17–20). She seems to be 'secondary' not only as a result of her gender, but also in comparison to her sibling:

> Her tresses showed a richer mass,
>   Her eyes looked softer than my own,
> Her figure had a statelier height,
>   Her voice a tenderer tone.

(ll. 13–16)

This superior femininity is matched by an equally harmonious ideological fit between the sister and the feminine ideal. The older sister, by contrast, is all fire to her sister's calm water, and when she reads Homer the fire is fanned:

> 'He stirs my sluggish pulse like wine,
>   He melts me like the wind of spice,
> Strong as strong Ajax' red right hand,
>   And grand like Juno's eyes.'

(ll. 29–32)

The imaginative and visceral stimulation provided by reading Homeric sagas brings home the limitations in contemporary society. Such a perception was a common Victorian view in the 1850s, with idealized Greek culture being perceived, as Matthew Arnold put it, to exhibit 'the utmost energy of life...the most entire freedom', while modern times and modern works of art display 'Depression and *ennui*'.[23] Rossetti adds a gendered dimension to this wider cultural debate: not only is her speaker's response to reading Homer richly sensual as well as imaginative, but she also draws attention to the assumption that readers of Greek literature (or any other literature) are male by pointing out her own difference and its attendant frustrations. 'I cannot melt the sons of men', she complains, 'I cannot fire and tempest-toss' (ll. 33–4). Her unacceptable volatility seems interpretable only as a fault or flaw, for 'blank life' (l. 70) offers no opportunity for female 'heroic strength' (l. 116), for physical expression of the energy she articulates. (In 1854 Rossetti volunteered to go to the Crimea with Florence Nightingale's nursing team, but was refused on account of her youth and thus deprived of 'heroic' possibilities.) In place of heroic action, the speaker of 'The Lowest Room' is supposed to content herself with embroidery, though her contempt for this activity and its end results is clear. She fantasizes that Greek women's weaving was more fulfilling and told a better tale than her own efforts:

> 'Or, look again, dim Dian's face
>   Gleamed perfect thro' the attendant night;
> Were not such better than those holes
>   Amid that waste of white?'

(ll. 77–80)

Like Elizabeth Barrett Browning's Aurora Leigh, Rossetti's speaker sees no value in culturally approved feminine productions. But where Aurora protests that women spend time making things that are useless or get in the way, it is the issue of representational limitation that lies at the heart of Rossetti's speaker's protest.[24] The embroidery offers itself as passive and virginal; it has no story to tell and its holes seem to signal vacuity.

All this protest does not go unchecked, however. As the poem proceeds, the Homeric pagan frame is superseded by Christianity at the instigation of the righteous sister, whose discourse aligns self-sacrificing femininity with Christ-like sacrifice for humanity. What is the appeal of Homer and his gods, she asks, 'To us who learn of Christ?' (l. 156). The aligning of Christ's position with feminine subjectivity, seen in its most radical and heroic form in *Goblin Market*, is frequently invoked by Rossetti as both lesson and palliative to resistant women. In *Seek and Find* she writes that, 'In many points the feminine lot copies very closely the voluntarily assumed position of our Lord and Pattern', citing obedience, subordination, the serving of others, and suffering in order to bring forth fruit as examples (*SF* 30–1). In 'The Lowest Room', as in *Seek and Find*, the virtues of self-abnegation are expounded through Christ as model and they persuade the previously rebellious speaker of their worthiness:

> Not to be first: how hard to learn
> That lifelong lesson of the past;
> Line graven on line and stroke on stroke;
> But, thank God, learned at last.
>
> (ll. 265–8)

The metaphors adopted for the 'lesson' are linguistic, but 'stroke' carries violent suggestions of flagellation, indicating the ferocity of the rebellious speaker's struggle to embrace feminine submission. One of the sacrifices she seems to have to make is her imagination, for she becomes increasingly entranced by her sister's superior femininity and Christian spirit, until she cannot keep her attention on the book she has chosen to 'read and dream' (l. 209) and it slides 'noiseless to the velvet floor' (l. 222). The movement towards a Christian/feminine position thus appears to necessitate or generate a rejection of texts liable to stir the pulse. As Rossetti later declared in *Letter and Spirit* (1883):

> how shall a heart preserve its purity if once the rein be given to imagination; if vivid pictures be conjured up, and stormy or melting emotions indulged?...For the books we now forbear to read, we shall one day be endued with wisdom and knowledge...For the pictures from which we turn, we shall gaze unabashed on the Beatific Vision. (*LS* 101–4)

It is in keeping with these deliberately blinkered attitudes that the imaginatively and sensually provocative world of classical literature with its polytheistic possibilities is banished. Again, as in *Goblin Market*, we see the gap that separates feminine perfection from creative power.

Like *Goblin Market* and 'Hero', 'The Lowest Room' ends with a projection into the future. The sisters are now twenty years older, the younger happily married and a mother. The speaker, however, is alone, living in her 'own world of interests, | Much felt but little shown' (ll. 263–4). The overtly stated self-suppression is notable here, for, while the speaker might have accepted her secondary status and learned patience despite the 'tedious' years (l. 270), she never manages to oust entirely the subversive, rebellious impulse so in evidence at the start of the poem. What takes place is both a confession that hidden feelings exist and a linguistic deferral to the afterlife 'When all deep secrets shall be shown, | And many last be first' (ll. 279–80). Crossing over into the eternal world is seen to bring about an inversion of the gender roles that dominate Victorian society: 'The rule is prominence for the husband, retiredness for the wife', writes Rossetti in *Letter and Spirit*, 'nevertheless, the Source and Author of all rule once emphatically declared, "Many that are first shall be last; and the last first"' (*LS* 57).

The chiastic formulation quoted in *Letter and Spirit* has its sources in Matthew 19: 30, Mark 10: 31, and Luke 13: 30. It is one that Rossetti returns to again and again, and it is this biblical dictum that is behind her constant call to occupy the 'lowest place' on earth (l. 271), for, if the first are last, then being assigned to the lowest place is the best assignation there can be. The paradox of this is that, while such a standpoint drastically undermines Rossetti's feminist resistance, it seems to be born of it. The limitations and frustrations of life are rendered bearable by imagining a place beyond them, by believing that, along with the woman clothed with the sun in *Revelation*, about whom Rossetti writes in *The Face of the Deep*, feminine subjects will, 'from the lowest place', go 'up higher' (*FD* 310).

The abandonment of engagement with the material world cannot but weaken the protests that erupt in poems such as 'The Lowest Room'. Notwithstanding such refusal to pursue issues in the field of the social, however, Rossetti's texts often highlight the tension between reflexive and referential aspects of language, and in the process problematize the division between absolute categories of material and noumenal. In 'The Lowest Room' we are told that 'all deep secrets shall be shown', gleaning that this projected exposure is to occur in a future not only beyond the poem but also beyond the world. But because the secrets issue from earthly existence and we have been party to the speaker's private feelings earlier in the poem, we are given at least partial access to the content of those 'deep secrets' which the poem pretends will only posthumously be revealed. Thus we are placed in a position which straddles two dimensions, for Rossetti's words both refer to a domain 'beyond', and function reflexively by worrying at the world circumscribed by language itself, within which feminine identity is written and silenced. The noumenal is not entirely inaccessible, since its content has been predetermined; rather it is a utopian representational space – a fantasy – finally inseparable from the phenomenal world which is both its shadow and its progenitor.

'The Lowest Room' was originally entitled 'A fight over the body of Homer', and the text is a veritable battleground, however placid its resolution may seem. Like *Goblin Market*, its struggle is not just about feminine roles and permissible activity for female bodies; it is also about representational possibilities for women artists. It asks what stories can be told, what can be written on the 'waste of white'? The emotional movement it charts, from resistance to restraint, from barely suppressed anger to manufactured peace, seems to point to a conservative resolution. But this movement, as we have seen, is replicated in numerous other poems, and the very repetition of such a pattern testifies to the failure of the project itself. The narratives keep having to be written because the storytellers will not be quiet and will not die. However much Rossetti's speakers seem to desire freedom from life and language, they continually mark their involvement in both by returning, over and over again, to the story.

3

Spirit

To give, to give, not to receive,
  I long to pour myself, my soul,
Not to keep back or count or leave
  But king with king to give the whole:
I long for one to stir my deep –
  I have had enough of help and gift –
  I long for one to search and sift
Myself, to take myself and keep.

You scratch my surface with your pin;
  You stroke me smooth with hushing breath; –
Nay pierce, nay probe, nay dig within,
  Probe my quick core and sound my depth.
You call me with a puny call,
  You talk, you smile, you nothing do;
  How should I spend my heart on you,
My heart that so outweighs you all?

Your vessels are by much too strait;
  Were I to pour you could not hold,
Bear with me: I must bear to wait
  A fountain sealed thro' heat and cold.

('The heart knoweth its own bitterness', (*PP* 53, ll. 25–44))

'The heart knoweth its own bitterness' is startling in its assertion of self and its criticisms of the patronizing superficiality of ordinary romantic relations. Rossetti, doubtless aware of the poem's outspoken and erotic content, suppressed the original text composed in 1857, only publishing a radically modified version in 1885, entitled '"Whatsoever is right, that shall ye receive"' (*CP* ii. 267). The unrevised poem is, however, much more interesting and intense in its charting of the process by which frustration generates first repression and then redirection of libidinous energy towards Christ. In common with many of Rossetti's explicitly devotional writings, which form the focus of this chapter, 'The heart knoweth its own bitterness' is insistent, challenging, and unexpected.

The speaker of 'The heart knoweth its own bitterness' makes it clear that she has multiple desires, that she wants both to give and to receive, to 'pour herself' and to be penetrated. She articulates a wish for equality and reciprocity seemingly impossible in Victorian culture, where human men appear hopelessly fixed in sexual attitude: their 'vessels' cannot 'hold' the flood of female sexuality, and so the speaker's 'fountain' must remain virginally 'sealed' until self can join other in heavenly plenitude. Only a fantasized Christ appears not to insist on a 'strait vessel' as regards sexuality, only He can match the speaker's passionate depths, and only with Christ can the ideal interpenetrative union occur:

> Not in this world of hope deferred,
>
> . . . .
>
> Here harvests fail, here breaks the heart;
> There God shall join and no man part,
> I full of Christ and Christ of me.

(ll. 49, 54–6).

DEVOTED LOVERS

The sentiments of 'The heart knoweth its own bitterness' connect it to other devotional poems by Rossetti which imagine the self in a spousal relation to Christ. These texts insert themselves into a long tradition of devotional poetry which uses the figure of marriage to signify union between devotee and divine. As John Keble puts it in his essay 'Sacred Poetry' (1825), there is 'the very highest warrant for the analogy which subsists between conjugal and divine love'.[1] The source text to which Keble refers is The Song of Solomon, the most erotic piece of writing in the Bible.

In common with mystical writers before her, Rossetti exploits the potential inherent in The Song of Solomon by not remaining tied to the traditional Christian allegorical frame wherein the Song's amatory register is interpreted as the love of Christ for His Church. Rossetti re-personalizes the love song, using its words to depict the desired union, offering the Song's words as consolation to her often dejected speakers and reproducing the intensely intimate tone of the Song itself. Notwithstanding the fantasy of 'The heart knoweth its own bitterness', however, Rossetti cannot always cast off the gendered power dynamics that operate ostensibly in the rejected earthly world. At the end of 'Old and New Year Ditties' (*PP* 66), Christ speaks to the depressed and suffering speaker of the poem, promising final release:

> Tho' I tarry, wait for Me, trust Me, watch and pray.
> Arise, come away, night is past and lo it is day,
> My love, My sister, My spouse, thou shalt hear Me say.
> Then I answered: Yea.

> (3, ll. 23–6)

Christ's terms of address are drawn directly from The Song of Solomon, but his promise operates in a particular way as He encourages the speaker to 'wait', 'watch', and 'pray', shoring up her faith but at the same time endorsing a conventional ideology of appropriate feminine behaviour. If the speaker is ultimately to be betrothed, patience and passivity are necessary: the promise acts also as an erotic encouragement to her to yearn but not to move. He takes his time – 'Tho' I tarry' – while she waits, reproducing the highly conventional erotic model that was subverted in 'The Prince's Progress' by the Princess dying, her spirit as it were refusing to wait any longer for this teasing, dallying lover.

In Rossetti's devotional poetry, however, wait one must, and, just as the Princess is herself unable to exert control over her situation and is dependent on a man for the possibility of salvation, so Rossetti's speakers must keep 'Wings folded close' until Christ calls. The impatience voiced in 'The heart knoweth its own bitterness' is, ideally, muted into a calm acceptance of the unknown divine will governing life and death. In 'Whitsun Tuesday' (*CP* ii. 234) the gold and silver wings of the soul are folded 'yet ready to unfold' (l. 11), 'When Thou shalt say, "Spouse, sister, love and dove, | Come hither, sit with Me upon My throne"' (ll. 12–14). At times the endless waiting seems to affect the female suppliant adversely, as in 'Thy fainting spouse, yet still Thy spouse' (*CP* ii. 208), which portrays a woman failing to sustain strength:

> Thy fainting spouse, yet still Thy spouse;
>> Thy trembling dove, yet still Thy dove;
> Thine own by mutual vows,
>> By mutual love.
>
> Recall Thy vows, if not her vows;
>> Recall Thy Love, if not her love:
> For weak she is, Thy spouse,
>> And tired, Thy dove.

(ll. 1–8)

In this plaintive, intimate poem the vulnerable woman seeks assurance and strength from the divine bridegroom who remains beyond both woman and poem. Rossetti emphasizes through repetition the reciprocal commitment that binds self and Christ, while she also emphasizes the difference between the 'fainting', 'trembling', 'weak', and 'tired' self (where all but the latter term directly connote femininity) and the stable, strong Christ. An important aspect of the spousal relation Rossetti depicts is the otherness of Christ, a condition doubled by the fact that Christ is both divine and male. Whereas in the passage from *Letter and Spirit* quoted in the previous chapter the feminine lot was compared to Christ's position on earth, such likeness disappears when Christ is figured in the divine state which is His 'proper place'.

Though Rossetti's devotional poems are, for the most part, moderately rather than ecstatically sensual, they display the characteristic amorous tension of mystical texts which depict the soul's union with Christ. 'Advent Sunday' (*CP* ii. 211) registers typically unequivocal sensual intimacy: 'His Hands are Hands she knows, she knows His Side' (l. 9), and depicts the tender union and rapture to come:

> His Eyes are as a Dove's, and she's Dove-eyed;
> He knows His lovely mirror, sister, Bride.
>
> He speaks with Dove-voice of exceeding love,
> And she with love-voice of an answering Dove.

(ll. 14–17)

In *The Face of the Deep*, Rossetti writes that 'Eve, the representative woman, received as part of her sentence "desire" ... Many women attain their heart's desire: many attain it not. Yet are these latter no losers if they exchange desire for aspiration, the corruptible for the incorruptible' (*FD* 312). The distinction Rossetti draws here between desire and aspiration is crucial to her own sense of the difference between focusing on earthly, material, and physical dimensions and looking towards the heavenly transcendent domain of the soul. Exchanging or transferring desire into fervent spiritual aspiration is recommended, then, but is Rossetti's distinction between the two terms sustainable?

The metaphor of marriage evident in The Song of Solomon, together with the sensual language of that text, blends rather than separates human and divine love. The language of Rossetti's devotional poetry reproduces such blending, so, *pace* the author's distinction, it is not possible to discern any real differences between a lexicon of desire and a lexicon of aspiration: just as The Song of Solomon brings together the physical and the unattainable transcendent, so Rossetti's texts yoke the corporeal and the spiritual. The language of scripture, upon which Rossetti depends heavily in her devotional poetry, makes a great deal of reference to the body and physical experience. Drawing on scriptural texts guarantees propriety, but the ready-made lexicon of scripture also allows for a more direct and immediate representation of the physical than is usual in Victorian women's literary texts. It is not only *Goblin Market* that features stark, violent, and uncompromising images of corporeality; in writing of Christ, Rossetti writes also of hunger, thirst, bleeding, cuts, 'wounds and bruises and putrifying sores', as she puts it in *Annus Domini* (p. 32). In poems such as '"Thou, God, seest me"', '"Behold the Man!"', '"Of Him That Was Ready to Perish"', '"The Love of Christ Which Passeth Knowledge"', '"Zion Said"', and 'The Three Enemies' (*CP* ii. 190, 153, 152; i. 66; iii. 245; *PP* 25), bodies are depicted as penetrable and/or penetrated, secreting, exposed, in pain, or mutilated. And apprehending the body is imperative: 'Shall Christ hang on the Cross, and we not look?' ('"Behold the Man!"', l. 1). Rossetti's devotional speakers are exceedingly assertive in the articulation of their desire; they emphasize both the necessity of a female gaze and the pleasures of being looked upon: 'Ah me, that I should be | Exposed and open evermore to Thee! –' begins '"Thou, God, seest me"', registering the wish to have no veil shielding Christ's face but to be exposed to his all-consuming, all-absorbing, and ultimately annihilating gaze.

Religious faith was the strongest force in Rossetti's life, and her devotional writings illustrate the depth and magnitude of her belief in all sorts of subtle as well as more obvious ways. The energy and drive of devotional desire are marked in the sonnet beginning 'Lord, dost Thou look on me, and will not I | Launch out my heart to Heaven to look on Thee?' (*CP* ii. 207, ll. 1–2), where the propulsive force of the verb 'Launch' signals the importance of reciprocity – the speaker strives to love God as much as He loves her – and the repetition of 'look' signals the importance of sight as a metaphor of communion. In this poem, as in 'The heart knoweth its own bitterness', devotional desire is again specifically contrasted with earthly love, which pales by comparison, so that by the end of the sonnet the speaker is appealing to Christ to grant her the wisdom, sight, and love which will allow her to be with 'Him' rather than 'him' (l. 4):

> Lord, dost Thou look on me, and will not I
>   Launch out my heart to Heaven to look on Thee?
>   Here if one loved me I should turn to see,
> And often think on him and often sigh,
> And by a tender friendship make reply
>   To love gratuitous poured forth on me,

(ll. 1–6)

The reserve, restraint and guardedness that characterize lines 3–6 are starkly contrasted to the tone of the sonnet's passionate opening couplet. The speaker is not as hostile towards earthly love as in 'The heart knoweth its own bitterness', but she makes it clear that her affections extend only to considerate regard and polite exchanges. Effective rebuffs are implied here too, for, as in her witty, '"No, Thank You, John"' (*PP* 74), Rossetti's speaker seems willing to offer 'friendship for you if you like; but love,– | No, thank you, John' (ll. 31–2).

Rossetti wrote devotional poetry throughout her life, but as she matured she turned more and more of her attention to her faith. She wrote literally hundreds of devotional poems, which range widely in form, focus, and feeling; she always included specifically religious lyrics in her poetic volumes, but her final collection, *Verses* (1893), is entirely devotional, and between 1874 and 1892 she published six long religious prose works.

Throughout her later years Rossetti suffered from acute physical illness. She was rarely physically well at any time in her life, but in 1872 she was diagnosed as suffering from Graves's disease (exophthalmic bronchole), which as well as being a serious condition was also physically disfiguring, producing the bulging eyes and swollen, puffy appearance evident in photographs of the older Rossetti. The poet had always been exceedingly shy in public situations, but the effect of her illness made her more socially reticent than ever. 'I am weak, and less ornamental than society may justly demand,' she wrote to William Michael in 1871 (*LCR* i. 380, Letter 459).

Rossetti remained single and, so far as we know, a virgin until the end of her life. Although a proposal of marriage was made by her timid, scholarly friend Charles Cayley in 1866, 'No, thank you' was Rossetti's response, for the possibility of marriage seems, by the mid-1860s, to have been closed off and independence deemed preferable. Rossetti did sustain a very close friendship with Cayley to the end of his life, however, and was not nearly as reclusive in her later years as has often been supposed. As a well-known, respected author, she received numerous requests and invitations, and she sustained literary connections as well as friendships and family ties. She corresponded with younger women poets such as Katharine Tynan and Lisa Wilson, who both became friends, maintained her closeness with the Heimanns, a Jewish family whom the Rossettis had known for years, and affectionately fulfilled her role of aunt to William's children. She kept herself actively involved in the world through her support for social causes, and above all focused her energies on her own work, the religious nature of which helped her to endure not only her own physical suffering but also the devastating losses of those closest to her.

It is perhaps a bitter irony that the poet who wrote so much about, and seemingly yearned for, death from her teenage years onwards should outlive all but her brother William Michael. Maria died in 1876, Dante Gabriel, after a painful period of drug addiction, acute paranoia, and depression, in 1882. Rossetti lost Charles Cayley in 1883, her mother Frances in 1886, and she nursed aunts Charlotte and Eliza (with whom she and Frances had resided since 1876), until their deaths in 1890 and 1893. All of these were terrible losses, but none more so than her mother, with whom Rossetti had so far lived all her life and to whom she was deeply attached. In a letter written just after her mother's death, she wrote: 'I have been grieved before but never so desolate as now.'[2]

The effect of multiple bereavements and intense physical suffering was to turn Rossetti's mind and imagination more determinedly than ever towards spiritual rather than material life. Her religion's assurance of an afterlife may partially have alleviated the pain of her increasingly enforced solitude. Solitariness, however, is not a condition confined to Rossetti's later years or writings; rather, it is a state of being that is crucial to her sense of poetic identity. From her earliest writings onwards, she represents women alone, and her depictions of female solitude importantly revise dominant cultural expectations about the 'plight' of single women. The status of 'virgin' is crucial to Rossetti's revisions, for, whereas the dominant view of nineteenth-century culture was that mature virgins were unfortunate spinsters, in this unpredictable writer's work, spinsters are exalted as privileged virgins.

VIRGINS

She whose heart is virginal abides aloft and aloof in spirit. In spirit she oftentimes kneels rather than sits, or prostrates herself more readily than she kneels, associated by love with Seraphim, and echoing and swelling the 'Holy, Holy, Holy,' of their perpetual adoration. Her spiritual eyes behold the King in His beauty; wherefore she forgets, by comparison, her own people and her father's house. Her Maker is her Husband, endowing her with a name better than of sons and of daughters. His Presence and His right hand are more to her than that fulness of joy and those pleasures which flow from them. For His sake rather than for its own she longs for Paradise; she craves the gold of that land less because it is good than because it is His promised gift to her. She loves Him with all her heart and soul and mind and strength; she is jealous that she cannot love Him more; her desire to love Him outruns her possibility, yet by outrunning enlarges it. She contemplates Him, and abhors herself in dust and ashes. She contemplates Him, and forgets herself in Him ... The air she breathes is too rare and keen for grosser persons; they mark the clouds which involve her feet, but discern not those early and late sunbeams which turn her mists to rainbows and kindle her veiled head to a golden glory. (*LS* 91–2)

In this revealing passage, the special qualities of virginal identity are expounded: devotion and desire for God are portrayed as all-consuming in their passion, even to the point of the virgin being 'jealous that she cannot love Him more'. The privilege and special quality of the virginal condition are made clear in the distinction between her and those 'grosser persons' who see only the most base examples of her being (her spinsterhood, perhaps), and do not perceive her radiance.

Immediately following this passage in *Letter and Spirit* is a companion account of the identity of wife, which is 'not in unison' with, but supposedly complements, the role of virgin. There is no doubt, however, where the authorial sympathy lies. The wife 'sees not face to face, but as it were in a glass darkly. Every thing, and more than all every person, and most of all the one best beloved person, becomes her mirror wherein she beholds Christ and her shrine wherein she serves Him' (*LS* 92). Taking the role of wife means accepting that the connection to Christ is always refracted through others, whereas the virgin enjoys an unmediated relationship with the divine; she loves Christ 'without let or hindrance through time and through eternity' (*AD* 181). Though Rossetti admits in *Letter and Spirit* that each 'vocation' has its dangerous temptations – for the wife a tendency to 'worship and serve the creature more than the Creator' and for the virgin a tendency 'to become narrow, self-centred' (*LS* 94) – the perils of virginity do not emerge as a cause for concern or focus for criticism in her writings to anything like the same degree as does the role of wife, the figure depicted so cuttingly as a 'fattened bee' in 'A Triad'.

The virgin is privileged, then, though she is not herself divine. Rossetti's Anglican faith kept her at a distance from the Mariolatry of Catholicism and on no occasion does she allow the virgin to intrude on the sacred Holy Trinity. Her poems 'Feast of the Annunciation' and 'Herself a rose, who bore the Rose' (*CP* ii. 238), which appeared sequentially in *A Pageant, and Other Poems*, both address the differences between Christ's human mother and the Divine Son. 'Feast of the Annunciation' begins with the question, 'Whereto shall we liken this Blessed Mary Virgin?' (l. 1), and responds to the question thus:

> Lily we might call her, but Christ alone is white;
> Rose delicious, but that Jesus is the one Delight;
> Flower of women, but her Firstborn is mankind's one flower:
> He the Sun lights up all moons thro' their radiant hour.

(ll. 3–6)

Similarly, 'Herself a rose...' takes pains to separate the laudable human virtues of Mary from the divinity of her child:

> Herself a rose, who bore the Rose,
>
> .   .   .   .   .   .
>
> Lily herself, she bore the one
>   Fair Lily; sweeter, whiter, far
> Than she or others are:
>
> .   .   .   .   .   .
>
> She gracious, He essential Grace,
> He was the Fountain, she the rill:

(ll. 1, 6–8, 11–12)

The final stanza makes the humanity of Mary clear, for she is seen to be like any other mortal person who must practise 'hope and love and faith' (l. 18) to join her Son in heavenly communion. The invocation of The Song of Solomon at the end of the poem emphasizes this, for Christ says 'Dove, | Spouse, Sister, Mother' (ll. 19–20) to any of his deserving spiritual brides, not just his human mother. Mary may be 'Blessed among women, highly favoured' ('Feast of the Annunciation', l. 7), but Rossetti insists that this is the limit of her privilege.

If the virginal state is specially blessed, it is also preferable to marriage in the independence and self-sufficiency it allows a female subject. Although Rossetti's overt claims about the value of virginity belong to her later work, throughout her career there is evidence of attitudes that lead directly to her mature perspective. 'The Solitary Rose' (CP iii. 103), written when Rossetti was just 16, privileges celibate independence over sexual relation and in the process also revises a common poetic convention:

> O happy Rose, red Rose, that bloomest lonely
>   Where there are none to gather while they love thee;
> That art perfumed by thine own fragrance only,
>   Resting like incense round thee and above thee; –
> Thou hearest nought save some pure stream that flows,
>   O happy Rose.

What tho' for thee no nightingales are singing?
    They chant one eve, but hush them in the morning.
Near thee no little moths and bees are winging
    To steal thy honey when the day is dawning; –
Thou keep'st thy sweetness till the twilight's close,
        O happy Rose.

Then rest in peace, thou lone and lovely flower;
    Yea be thou glad, knowing that none are near thee
To mar thy beauty in a wanton hour,
    And scatter all thy leaves, nor deign to wear thee.
Securely in thy solitude repose,
        O happy Rose.

(ll. 1–18)

Familiar here is the representation of lovers as potentially voracious, destructive, and unreliable. Rossetti slips up with her natural metaphor in the final stanza, making the human context to which she alludes transparent: it is not bees or birds, but people who 'wear' flowers. Nevertheless it is not the threat of others that is as significant in this poem as the appreciation of the autonomous privacy of the rose. The state which the rose is seen to occupy, secure in its solitude, possibly lonely but certainly self-sufficient, even auto-erotically satisfied through being perfumed by 'its own fragrance', is not a conventional model for non-conventional Victorian women.

Nor is it ordinarily the case that a rose should be invoked in order that its amatory associations may be written against, but this is precisely what Rossetti does. The rose is an over-determined signifier of love and female sexuality, and, when depicted, it inevitably draws centuries of poetic tradition along with it. But Rossetti inverts the entire paradigm, by celebrating the rose's *lack* of romantic attachment. Furthermore, her speaker's appreciation of the rose's celibate autonomy distances her from innumerable male poets who have sung the beauty of the rose, thereby redoubling the effect of the revision, for both object (rose) and subject (speaker) are recast – the rose as admirably autonomous, the speaker as calmly appreciative and protective rather than possessive or fetishistic. A feminine poetics is created, where the value of both the speaker's perception and that of the solitary rose itself is brought to the fore. Rossetti creates a safe space for female sexuality, not only banishing Blake's 'invisible worm' who destroys his 'Sick Rose' with its 'dark secret love', but rejecting also the voyeuristic, sadistic gaze that sees such menace at work.

The dignity and self-possession of a feminine identity founded only upon itself, rather than in relation to another human being, is much in evidence throughout Rossetti's work. But while the construction of virginity may have biblical precedents which many female mystics, visionaries, and other kinds of women writers have drawn upon to shore up their authority, such an identity is not without its feminine limitations. Keble voices a standard Christian perspective when he declares: 'What control of speech, what modesty in their whole conduct of life, they must exhibit who would be held to merit the title of virgin'.[3] Rossetti would agree, and thus she has many subtle strategies for appearing to control her speech despite writing hundreds of thousands of words across three score years. Her devotional works are routinely peppered with apologias and self-deprecatory statements and she often genuflects to the patriarchal authority of her Church and its particular prejudice against women daring to engage in theology or hermeneutics.

At the same time, however, Rossetti's prose is frequently subversive of many of the Church's conservative positions on gender. In *The Face of the Deep*, she writes,

> To expound prophecy lies of course beyond my power, and not within my wish. But the symbolic forms of prophecy being set before all eyes, must be so set for some purpose: to investigate them may not make us wise as serpents; yet ought by promoting faith, fear, hope, love, to aid in making us harmless as doves. 'Write the vision, and make it plain upon tables, that he may run that readeth it': – God helping us, we all great and small can and will run. (*FD* 195)

There is real defiance here as well as a genuine wish to do what Rossetti considers right by God. This is a typically tricky passage, full of twists and turns which obscure the radicalism of what is being said. Rossetti resists the power of the clergy and their sole claim to be interpreters of scripture, using biblical quotation against the authorities to assert the right of 'all great and small' to read and interpret for themselves. She denies the desire or ability to expound prophecy, but proceeds to claim that all have both right and capacity to do just that. She twists the meaning of 'wise' by alluding to serpents, thus suggesting the potential dangerousness of those who claim to have special wisdom, and then furthers her argument that biblical exegesis should be open to all, suggesting it promotes the devotional virtues of 'faith, fear, hope [and] love'.

What is especially significant about this passage is that it appears immediately after an invocation of the famous Pauline prohibition on women teaching: 'St. Paul has written: "Let the woman learn in silence with all subjection. But I suffer not a woman to teach." Yet elsewhere he wrote: "I call to remembrance the unfeigned faith…which dwelt first in thy grandmother Lois, and thy mother Eunice."' (FD 195). Here Rossetti uses her extensive knowledge of biblical texts to make Paul's own words work against himself. Reminding him, and her readers, of his second epistle to his son Timothy, she points out that the faith of Lois and Eunice indubitably influenced and socialized. Thus the women were most effective teachers. This entire passage in The Face of the Deep takes unequivocal issue with gender restrictions and skilfully manipulates scriptural language to undermine patriarchal precedents, without at any time deviating from its adherence to Christian principles. Within the parameters of her chosen discourse, Rossetti's revisions are radical.

A similar movement occurs earlier in The Face of the Deep, when Rossetti says, 'Far be it from me to think to unfold mysteries or interpret prophecies'. She then makes a virtue of ignorance: 'But I trust that to gaze in whatever ignorance on what God reveals, is so far to do His will. If ignorance breed humility, it will not debar from wisdom. If ignorance betake itself to prayer, it will lay hold on grace' (FD 146). Once more, knowing little is presented as no barrier to the apprehension of God's message, thus the right to interpret is opened up to all. The readership of Rossetti's devotional works was primarily female, and there are many points at which her use of collective pronouns and terms of address allude to this fact, as in her reminder of the power of 'We who are weak' (recalling the 'We' of 'In an Artist's Studio') in a specifically gendered context in Time Flies. 'We who are weak', predictably, turn out to be strong, and vice versa: 'the "strong" of one sentence will be the "weak" of another' (TF 57). Rossetti's aim here is to encourage women to make use of all their resources, rather than associate the 'weaker sex' with the helplessness conventionally ascribed to it in patriarchal culture.

The *Face of the Deep* passage in which Rossetti makes a virtue of ignorance continues to argue, implicitly, that women have not just a right but also a spiritual duty to contemplate that which will 'deepen awe, and stir up desire by a contemplation of things inevitable, momentous, transcendent'. Using the analogy of eagles and doves for men and women, Rossetti claims it 'would be a sore mistake on the dove's part were she to say, Because I am not the eagle I am not a sun bird, and so were to cut herself off from the sun's gracious aspect' (*FD* 146). Thus does the poet–sage direct advice to her readers, despite her earlier disclaimers of authority; and she has a right to do so, because it is made abundantly clear in this and other works that she is very far from 'ignorant' when it comes to scriptural knowledge.

Rossetti's seizing of authority, interspersed with acceptably feminine shows of modesty, humility, and simple faith (all of which qualities Rossetti highlights as important Christian virtues, thus shoring up the status of women even in the process of placating masculinist perspectives), may partially be accounted for with reference to movements within the Anglican Church. The Anglican sisterhoods set up in the nineteenth century were significant in defining a space for women to lead separate religious lives and to organize themselves autono-mously.[4] Furthermore, they encouraged debate and discussion between women and asserted women's right to live in celibacy. Such intellectual and sexual challenges to mainstream patri-archal society did not go unnoticed, and objections were raised regarding the threat sisterhoods represented to the Victorian family.[5] Nevertheless, the model they offered could not but have been encouraging to Rossetti for it gave authority to her as a single, celibate, and devout woman, offering a real alternative not only to the role of wife but also to that of 'rejected' woman in a heterosexual economy (even if it was Rossetti who in fact did the rejecting).

In a poem Rossetti wrote in 1849, originally entitled 'The End of the First Part' and later forming the second part of the triptych 'Three Stages' (*PP* 37), the speaker's poetic self-fashioning uses a convential metaphor to describe the place where she will abide. The poet–speaker describes the shattering of a dream and the necessity to 'pull down my palace that I built' and 'Dig up the pleasure-gardens of my soul' (ll. 9–10). In place of the sensual delights of the past, the speaker asserts that,

> . . . where my palace stood, with the same stone,
> I will uprear a shady hermitage;
> And there my spirit shall keep house alone,
> Accomplishing its age:

(ll. 21–4)

The poet builds herself her own convent, where she will live, alone and celibate, until 'the last lingering chime' (l. 28). Although there is no doubt that this involves very considerable sacrifice, entering one's own hermitage also provides protection and, unlike a real convent, does not necessitate surrendering the profession of poet. The shady hermitage also distances the woman writer from her male literary influences and gives her her own specific identity. Tearing down the palace and digging up the pleasure-gardens illustrate a rejection of the Romantic and Victorian poetic sensualism represented by Coleridge's 'pleasure-dome' in 'Kubla Khan' and Tennyson's 'Palace of Art'. Rossetti's poetic identity will be predicated on the same renunciation of worldly delights as that of her conventual sisters, and this, for the poet, will involve changing linguistic 'freedom to control' (l. 12). Such a poetics of reserve will be the equivalent of conventual asceticism.

Early in her poetic career, then, Rossetti appropriates the conventual model for the purpose of constructing her own, authoritative, poetic identity. In much later poems such an identity is still in place: the poet's sense of autonomous solitude is intact in 'The Thread of Life' (*PP* 228), a triptych of sonnets which contain important statements regarding Rossetti's sense of her poetic persona. In the first sonnet, the speaker is described as 'bound with the flawless band | Of inner solitude' (1, ll. 5–6). At the start of the second sonnet she declares: 'Thus am I mine own prison' (2, l. 1). The speaker is alienated from the 'merrymaking crew' (2, l. 9) who are at home in the world, but her isolated existence generates not existential despair but unequivocal self-assertion: 'I am not what I have nor what I do; | But what I was I am, I am even I' (2, ll. 13–14). This conception of self recalls the biblical proclamation 'I, even I, am the Lord' (Isa. 43: 11) and parallels a more elaborate statement of identity found in *The Face of the Deep*:

> Concerning Himself God Almighty proclaimed of old: 'I AM THAT I AM', and man's inherent feeling of personality seems in some sort to attest and correspond to this revelation: I who am myself cannot but be myself. I am what God has constituted me: so that however I may have modified myself, yet do I remain that same I; it is I who live, it is I who must die, it is I who must rise again at the last day...Who I was I am, who I am I am, who I am I must be for ever and ever.
>
> (FD 47)

This account of identity implies, among other things, that self-renunciation has its limits: if it is not possible to 'unself' oneself, there is a point beyond which feminine self-abnegation cannot reach. Indeed, in the final sonnet of 'The Thread of Life', a dramatic expansion of self-assurance takes place:

> Therefore myself is that one only thing
>   I hold to use or waste, to keep or give;
>   My sole possession every day I live,
> And still mine own despite Time's winnowing.
> Ever mine own, while moons and seasons bring
>   From crudeness ripeness mellow and sanative;
>   Ever mine own, till Death shall ply his sieve;
> And still mine own, when saints break grave and sing.
>
> (3, ll. 1–8)

Such assertion not only of self but of rights over the self could not come from a woman who had adopted what Emily Dickinson ironically calls the 'honourable Work | Of Woman, and of Wife'.[6] The 'I' of a wife is not her own at this point in history; rather she is legally bound to her husband to 'use or waste, to keep or give'. So once more the significance of Rossetti's single celibate status comes to the fore and provides her with an unparalleled autonomy. With this power, she chooses to give herself to 'Him Who gave Himself for me' (3, l. 9). She gives herself 'as king unto my King' (3, l. 9), a choice of phrase suggesting that the 'self' to which Rossetti refers is ultimately conceived as unrestricted by gender or sexuality. Union with Christ is cast here not in terms of a marriage of souls, but, as far as possible, as an elimination of difference. Though the masculine term 'king' is adopted for self-definition, this name signals the highest status any person can have on earth, and its proximity to 'King' draws attention to the oneness that Rossetti believes will occur after death. Such promised oneness is elsewhere invoked as a palliative to rebellious women: 'But if our proud waves will after all not be stayed ... by the limit of God's ordinance concerning our sex, one final consolation yet remains to careful and troubled hearts: in Christ there is neither male nor female, for we are all one (Gal.iii.28)' (SF 32). The passage from Galatians to which Rossetti refers has been invoked by Christian women throughout history in attempts to negotiate with patriarchal precepts. But the problem is that on earth sexual difference is insisted upon; thus any 'consolation' is empirically, if not spiritually, irrelevant and truly 'final' in so far as it can only be posthumous.

Nevertheless, imagining the suspension of sexual difference is politically a very significant gesture. We have seen that Rossetti makes use of all available possibilities in defining the relationship between her solitary women and the divine object of adoration. Christ may be unequivocally Other, indubitably masculine, a model of 'likeness' for the feminine, or a site where sexual difference disappears. Such fluidity is mirrored in the identities Rossetti creates for her speakers, who move in and out of socially prescribed roles, thus highlighting that such roles are not predetermined, fixed ontologies, but much more unstable and provisional subjectivities. It is the solitary, virginal status of Rossetti's speakers that makes such flexibility possible, because their marginality to the social order allows the articulation of perspectives at odds with the mainstream. The thresholds and borderlands, dream-states and twilight regions that Rossetti's speakers inhabit form the topography of this marginal place: hovering around the edges of normative psychosocial regions, they retain their autonomy and resist cultural absorption.

At times, Rossetti colludes with the misogynistic perspectives of scriptural texts which were, for her, divinely inspired and therefore not dismissable. Vanity and weakness in the face of temptation are often seen as the special flaws of women, and the female body and female sexuality sometimes figured as disgusting and depraved. 'Through Eve's lapse, weakness and shame devolved on woman as her characteristics' (FD 310), and 'a perverse rebellious woman because feminine not masculine is liable' to exhibit 'particular foulness, degradation, loathsome-

71

ness' (FD 400). 'The World' (PP 36) is personified as feminine on account of its satanic seductions and temptations:

> By day she wooes me, soft, exceeding fair:
> But all night as the moon so changeth she;
> Loathsome and foul with hideous leprosy
> And subtle serpents gliding in her hair.

(ll. 1–4)

Rossetti does not, then, avoid the Christian association of women with evil and wickedness. She acknowledges and at times reproduces it for the lessons she can glean from it, but her concern to 'adhere to a just weight, a just measure, even balances, a superhuman standard' (FD 271) in all dealings means that she will not go along with a patriarchal perception of women as *more* evil than men. 'Some have opined that a woman's wickedness even exceeds that of a man...But this point must stand over for decision to the Judgment of that Only Judge to whom each and all of us will one day stand or fall' (FD 400). Thus does Rossetti refute the authority of any human man to claim moral superiority over or to denigrate any woman. Thus does she also, simultaneously, refuse to argue the case further in the socio-political context of material existence.

'Earth is a race-course, not a goal', she declares in *The Face of the Deep*. 'Instead of mansions she pitches tents. Her nearest approach to a permanent abode is the grave' (FD 343). This perception of the impermanence of earthly life and its ultimate insignificance in comparison to 'Glowing, indestructible' heaven ('Earth and Heaven' (CP iii. 85, l. 22)) was unwavering in Rossetti's consciousness. Her spiritual life may be characterized by 'hungering and thirsting with a hunger and thirst which no earthly dainties could appease' (SF 145), while her work, in all its paradoxical, enigmatic, and careful voices, registers a parallel, unquenchable desire.

> Experience bows a sweet contented face,
>
> .   .   .   .
>
> While Hope, who never yet hath eyed the goal,
> With arms flung forth, and backward floating hair,
> Touches, embraces, hugs the invisible.

('Experience bows a sweet contented face' (CP ii. 251, ll. 1, 12–14))

Notes

PROLOGUE

1. Nicholas Shrimpton, 'New Spirits of the Age', review of *The Penguin Book of Victorian Verse*, ed. Daniel Karlin, *TLS*, 6 Feb. 1998, p. 6.

CHAPTER 1. MIND

1. Tractarians, so-called on account of a series of Tracts published in *The Times* newspaper between 1833 and 1841, defended the Church of England as a divine institution that should not be subordinated to the State and aimed to revive High Church traditions while remaining separate from the Roman Catholic Church. Key figures include John Keble and John Henry Newman. Tractarianism is also commonly referred to as the Oxford Movement.
2. Jan Marsh, *Christina Rossetti: A Literary Biography* (London: Jonathan Cape, 1994), 271.
3. W. David Shaw has an excellent essay examining the formal techniques by which Rossetti's poetry cultivates a sense of mystery. See 'Poet of Mystery: The Art of Christina Rossetti', in David A. Kent (ed.), *The Achievement of Christina Rossetti'* (Ithaca, NY: Cornell University Press, 1987), 23–56.
4. For a detailed examination of the Prince's pilgrimage and his failure correctly to interpret the symbolic signs he encounters, see Mary Arseneau, 'Pilgrimage and Postponement: Christina Rossetti's *The Prince's Progress*', *Victorian Poetry*, 32/3–4 (1994), 279–98.
5. See the Select Bibliography for reference to essays on *Goblin Market*. See also Dawn Henwood, 'Christian Allegory and Subversive Poetics: Christina Rossetti's *Prince's Progress* Re-examined', *Victorian Poetry*, 35/1 (1997), 83–94.
6. Caroline Norton, '"The Angel in the House" and "The Goblin Market"', *Macmillan's Magazine*, 8 (Sept. 1863), 402.

7. Antony H. Harrison's 'Introduction' to the Rossetti Centennial edition of *Victorian Poetry* reviews recent shifts in critical perception and points out the ways in which feminist and historicist criticism are revealing the 'intellectual complexity and critical power' of her work (*Victorian Poetry*, 32/3–4 (1994), 203–7).

8. Julia Kristeva, 'Psychoanalysis and the Polis', originally published in *Critical Inquiry*, 9, repr. in *The Kristeva Reader*, ed. Toril Moi (Oxford: Basil Blackwell, 1986), 301–20. This reference to the *Reader*, p. 304, emphasis in original.

9. Secondary revision refers to the reconstruction of a dream by the conscious mind, the effect of which is to form the dream into a narrative. See S. Freud, *The Interpretation of Dreams* (1900; Pelican Freud, 4 (Harmondsworth: Penguin, 1976; repr. 1991)), 633, and Freud's essay, 'Dreams' (1916; Pelican Freud, 1 (Harmondsworth: Penguin, 1973; repr. 1991)), 216–17.

10. For further discussion of storytelling strategies in *Speaking Likenesses*, see my essay, ' "All mouth and trousers": Christina Rossetti's Grotesque Bodies', in Isobel Armstrong and Virginia Blain (eds.), *Gender and Genre* (Basingstoke: Macmillan, 1998), ii. 292–312.

11. Quoted in Lewis Carroll, *The Annotated Snark*, ed. Martin Gardner (Harmondsworth: Penguin, 1962), 22.

12. The final suggestion is from Georgina Battiscombe (*Christina Rossetti: A Divided Life* (London: Constable, 1981), 109). Lona Mosk Packer claims that the 'prototype for the magnificent beast' is William Bell Scott (*Christina Rossetti* (Berkeley and Los Angeles: University of California Press, 1963), 94). Kathleen Jones suggests that the crocodile may be the Tzar of Russia, or William Morris, whom Dante Gabriel nicknamed 'The Prudent' (*Learning Not to be First: The Life of Christina Rossetti* (Moreton-in-Marsh: Windrush Press, 1991), 68–9). See *Rossetti Papers 1862 to 1870*, ed. W. M. Rossetti (London: Sands & Co., 1903), 67–9, for further family reference to 'My Dream' and to two drawings of crocodiles by Ernest Griset which Christina was given by her brothers in 1864.

13. Cora Kaplan, 'The Indefinite Disclosed: Christina Rossetti and Emily Dickinson', in *Sea Changes* (London: Verso, 1986), 109–110.

14. Freud, 'Dreams', 273.

15. Ibid., 274. See also Freud, *Jokes and their Relation to the Unconscious* (1905; Pelican Freud, 6 (Harmondsworth: Penguin, 1976; repr. 1991)), 61, 266, 230. Freud's distinction between jokes and dreams is suggestive. He says that a dream 'still remains a wish, even though one that has been made unrecognizable; a joke is developed play' (*Jokes*, 238). As far as Rossetti's poem is concerned, both definitions seem applicable.

16. Angela Carter, *Nothing Sacred* (London: Virago, 1982), 111.

17. Adam Phillips, *On Flirtation* (Faber & Faber, 1994), pp. xvii, xxiii.
18. Isobel Armstrong notes the symmetry of the first line in *Victorian Poetry: Poetry, Poetics and Politics* (London: Routledge, 1993), 358. Note that Marsh's edition mis-punctuates the first line of 'Winter: My Secret': there should be a colon at the end of line one, not a question mark.
19. Phillips argues that repetition creates the illusion of time having stopped and that flirtation is a way of playing for time (*On Flirtation*, 153, xix).
20. See Wim Tigges, *An Anatomy of Literary Nonsense* (Amsterdam: Rodopi, 1988).
21. See Marsh, *Christina Rossetti*, 258–64 and *passim*.
22. The most thorough examination of these aesthetic influences is Antony H. Harrison, *Christina Rossetti in Context* (Brighton: Harvester Press, 1988).
23. To be published in *LCR*, iii. Letter dated 14. 1886 [?January].
24. Steven Connor discusses Rossetti's play with meaning and meanings in '"Speaking Likenesses": Language and Repetition in Christina Rossetti's "Goblin Market"', *Victorian Poetry*, 22/4 (1984), 439–48. This brief article remains one of the most suggestive pieces of criticism on Rossetti's playful dealings with poetic language.
25. Jean-Jacques Lecercle, *Philosophy of Nonsense* (London: Routledge, 1994), 25.
26. See Harrison, *Christina Rossetti in Context*, 117.
27. For a somewhat different interpretation of 'After Death', examining the poem's relation to texts by Tennyson and Shakespeare, see Catherine Maxwell, 'The Poetic Context of Christina Rossetti's "After Death"', *English Studies*, 76/2 (1995), 143–55.
28. Linda Ruth Williams, *Critical Desire: Psychoanalysis and the Literary Subject* (London: Edward Arnold, 1995), 181.
29. See Jerome J. McGann, 'The Religious Poetry of Christina Rossetti', *Critical Inquiry*, 10 (1983), 127–44.
30. The quotation is from Angela Leighton, '"When I am dead, my dearest": The Secret of Christina Rossetti', *Modern Philology*, 87 (1990), 375. See also Linda E. Marshall, 'What the Dead are Doing Underground: Hades and Heaven in the Writings of Christina Rossetti', *Victorian Newsletter*, 72 (1987), 55–60, and Maxwell, 'Poetic Context', 150.
31. *Maud* was published two years before Rossetti's poem was composed.
32. *The Complete Poems of Emily Jane Brontë*, ed. C. W. Hatfield (New York: Columbia University Press, 1948), 56–7.
33. See Marsh, *Christina Rossetti*, 297.

CHAPTER 2. BODY

1. Ellen Proctor, *A Brief Memoir of Christina Rossetti* (London: SPCK, 1895), 66.
2. Mackenzie Bell, *Christina Rossetti: A Biographical and Critical Study* (London: Hurst & Blackett, 1898), 112.
3. Ibid.
4. There are some differences between Bell's and Marsh's transcriptions of the letters to Webster. An accurate version will be available in *LCR* ii.
5. See Angela Leighton, *Victorian Women Poets: Writing Against the Heart* (Hemel Hempstead: Harvester Wheatsheaf, 1992), 44, 37.
6. Rossetti does, however, allow Gabriel to edit the poem further, agreeing that he may 'suppress that "screech"' (*LCR* i. 239, Letter 264). Unfortunately no manuscript of the poem is known, so it is not possible to establish where such a cry of rage or outrage originally appeared.
7. See Jan Marsh, *Christina Rossetti: A Literary Biography* (London: Jonathan Cape, 1994), 89–97 and *passim*.
8. For a sound analysis of the relation between social conventions and fantasy literature, see T. E. Apter, *Fantasy Literature* (Basingstoke: Macmillan, 1982), 111.
9. Charles Dickens, 'Frauds on the Fairies', *Household Words*, 8/184 (5 Oct. 1853), 58.
10. Examples of such tales are included in Nina Auerbach and U. C. Knoepflmacher (eds.), *Forbidden Journeys: Fairy Tales and Fantasies by Victorian Women Writers* (Chicago: Chicago University Press, 1992).
11. Marina Warner (*From the Beast to the Blonde* (1994; repr. London: Vintage, 1995)) provides a wealth of information on women's crucial role in the dissemination of fairy stories in European culture from the Middle Ages to the present day.
12. Elizabeth K. Helsinger, 'Consumer Power and the Utopia of Desire: Christina Rossetti's "Goblin Market"' in Joseph Bristow (ed.), *Victorian Women Poets* (Basingstoke: Macmillan, 1995), 190.
13. See also Elizabeth Campbell, 'Of Mothers and Merchants: Female Economics in Christina Rossetti's "Goblin Market"', *Victorian Studies*, 33/3 (1990), 393–410, and Terrence Holt, '"Men sell not such in any town": Exchange in *Goblin Market*', *Victorian Poetry*, 28/1 (1990), 51–67, repr. in Tess Cosslett (ed.), *Victorian Women Poets* (London: Longman, 1996), 194–211, and Angela Leighton (ed.), *Victorian Women Poets: A Critical Reader* (Oxford: Basil Blackwell, 1996), 131–47.
14. For examples of works classifying fairy types, see Thomas Keightley,

The Fairy Mythology (London, 1828), or Archibald Maclaren, *The Fairy Family* (London, 1857).

15. See, for further reference, Leonard Barkan, *The Gods Made Flesh: Metamorphosis and the Pursuit of Paganism* (New Haven: Yale University Press, 1986), 14–15, and Elizabeth Truax, *Metamorphosis in Shakespeare's Plays* (Lampeter: Edwin Mellen Press, 1992), 3, 119, and *passim*.

16. Jack Zipes argues that this is a function of many fairy tales (*Breaking the Magic Spell: Radical Theories of Folk and Fairy Tales* (1979; repr. London: Routledge, 1992), 139).

17. 'Goblin Market – Ribald Classic', illustrated by Kinuko Craft, *Playboy*, 20 (1973), 115–19.

18. Adrienne Rich coined the phrase 'lesbian continuum' in her analysis of same-sex relations ('Compulsory Heterosexuality and Lesbian Existence', *Signs*, 5/4 (1980), 631–60).

19. 'Nick' is a violent tale of a greedy miser whose horrific metamorphic experiences transform him, finally, into a generous individual. It is notable that, whereas some ambivalence characterizes Hero's experience, in Nick's case metamorphosis is unequivocally used as punishment.

20. Cora Kaplan, 'Plenary Address', Feminist Criticism Conference, University of Exeter, 14 Apr. 1992.

21. Mikhail Bakhtin cites violations of verbal norms, as well as profanity and parody, as central to the disruptive spirit of carnival (*Problems of Dostoevsky's Poetics*, trans. R. W. Rotsel (Ann Arbor: Ardis, 1973), 96, 101, 104–5).

22. The model in question is Lizzie Siddal, who eventually died of a laudanum overdose.

23. Matthew Arnold, 'On the Modern Element in Literature' (1857), in *The Complete Prose Works of Matthew Arnold*, ed. R. H. Super (Ann Arbor: University of Michigan Press, 1960), i. 23, 32.

24. See Elizabeth Barrett Browning, *Aurora Leigh*, First Book, ll. 457–65. A widely available edition is edited by Cora Kaplan (London: The Women's Press, 1978).

CHAPTER 3. SPIRIT

1. John Keble, 'Sacred Poetry', *Quarterly Review*, 32 (1825), 221.

2. Letter to Lady Georgiana Mount-Temple (9 Apr. 1886). Autogr. MS. in Pierpont Morgan Library, New York. To be published in *LCR* iii.

3. John Keble, *Lectures on Poetry, 1832–1841*, trans. Edward Kershaw Francis (Oxford: Clarendon Press, 1912), ii. 86.

4. For discussion of Rossetti and Anglican sisterhoods, see Antony H.

Harrison, 'Christina Rossetti and the Sage Discourse of Feminist High Anglicanism', in Thaïs E. Morgan (ed.), *Victorian Sages and Cultural Discourse: Renegotiating Gender and Power* (New Brunswick, NJ: Rutgers University Press, 1990), 99–104.

5. See ibid. 98–100.
6. *Emily Dickinson: The Complete Poems*, ed. Thomas H. Johnson (London: Faber & Faber, 1970), no. 732, ll. 3–4.

Select Bibliography

WORKS BY CHRISTINA ROSSETTI

Poetry
Verses, printed privately (London: 1847).
Goblin Market and Other Poems (London: Macmillan, 1862).
The Prince's Progress and Other Poems (London: Macmillan, 1866).
Goblin Market, The Prince's Progress and Other Poems (London: Macmillan, 1875).
A Pageant and Other Poems (London: Macmillan, 1881).
Verses (London: SPCK, 1893).
New Poems, ed. W. M. Rossetti (London: Macmillan, 1896).
The Poetical Works of Christina Georgina Rossetti with Memoir and Notes, ed. W. M. Rossetti (London: Macmillan, 1904).
The Complete Poems of Christina Rossetti: A Variorum Edition, ed. R. W. Crump (3 vols.; Baton Rouge, La.: Louisiana State University Press, 1979–90).
Christina Rossetti: Poems and Prose, ed. Jan Marsh (London: Everyman, 1994). Select edition.
'Goblin Market – Ribald Classic', illustrated by Kinuko Craft, *Playboy*, 20 (1973), 115–19. Extracts from the poem.

Short Stories
Corrispondenzia Famigliare, in *The Bouquet from Marylebone Gardens*, printed privately (London: 1852).
Commonplace and Other Short Stories (London: F. S. Ellis, 1870).
Maude: A Story for Girls, ed. W. M. Rossetti (London: James Bowden, 1897).

Writing for Children
Sing-Song: A Nursery Rhyme Book (London: Routledge, 1872).
Speaking Likenesses (London: Macmillan, 1874).

Devotional Works

Annus Domini: A Prayer for Each Day of the Year (London: James Parker, 1874).

Seek and Find: A Double Series of Short Stories of the Benedicite (London: SPCK, 1879).

Called to Be Saints: the Minor Festivals Devotionally Studied (London: SPCK, 1881).

Letter and Spirit: Notes on the Commandments (London: SPCK, 1883).

Time Flies: A Reading Diary (London: SPCK, 1885).

The Face of the Deep: A Devotional Commentary on the Apocalypse (London: SPCK, 1892).

Rossetti family letters and diaries

Pre-Raphaelite Diaries and Letters, ed. W. M. Rossetti (London: Hurst & Blackett, 1900).

Rossetti Papers 1862 to 1870, ed. W. M. Rossetti (London: Sands & Co., 1903).

The Family Letters of Christina Georgina Rossetti, ed. W. M. Rossetti (London: Brown, Langham & Co., 1908).

Three Rossettis: Unpublished Letters to and from Dante Gabriel, Christina, William, ed. Janet Camp Troxell (Cambridge: Cambridge University Press, 1937).

The Rossetti–Macmillan Letters: Some 133 Unpublished Letters Written to Alexander Macmillan, F. S. Ellis, and Others, by Dante Gabriel, Christina, and William Michael Rossetti, 1861–1889, ed. Lona Mosk Packer (Berkeley and Los Angeles: University of California Press, and Cambridge: Cambridge University Press, 1963).

Letters of Dante Gabriel Rossetti, ed. O. Doughty and J. R. Wahl (4 vols.; Oxford: Clarendon Press, 1965–7).

The Owl and the Rossettis: Letters of Charles A. Howell and Dante Gabriel, Christina and William Michael Rossetti, ed. C. L. Cline (University Park, Pa.: Pennsylvania State University Press, 1978).

The Diary of W. M. Rossetti 1870–1873, ed. Odette Bornand (Oxford: Clarendon Press, 1987).

The Letters of Christina Rossetti, ed. Antony H. Harrison (4 vols.; Charlottesville, Va.: University Press of Virginia, 1997–).

BIOGRAPHICAL AND CRITICAL STUDIES

The focus here is on recent criticism. For early responses, a good initial source listing critical commentary from earliest reviews to 1973 is *Christina Rossetti: A Reference Guide*, ed. R. W. Crump (Boston: G. K. Hall,

1976). A subsequent bibliographical source is Jane Addison, 'Christina Rossetti Studies, 1974–1991: A Checklist and Synthesis', *Bulletin of Bibliography*, 52/1 (1995), 73–93.

Apostolos Cappadona, Diane, 'Oxford and the Pre-Raphaelites from the Perspective of Nature and Symbol', *Pre-Raphaelite Review*, 2/1 (1981), 90–110. Discusses Tractarian influence on Pre-Raphaelite representations, including poems by Rossetti.

Armstrong, Isobel, 'Christina Rossetti: Diary of a Feminist Reading', in Sue Roe (ed.), *Women Reading Women's Writing* (Brighton: Harvester Press, 1987), 117–37. A personal account of reading Rossetti in the light of feminist perspectives. Reprinted in Cosslett (ed.), *Victorian Women Poets*, 158–75.

—— *Victorian Poetry: Poetry, Poetics and Politics* (London: Routledge, 1993). Influential study; includes illuminating chapter on Rossetti and other Victorian women poets, reprinted in Bristow (ed.), *Victorian Women Poets*, 32–63, and Leighton (ed.), *Victorian Women Poets: A Critical Reader*, 245–76.

Arseneau, Mary, 'Incarnation and Interpretation: Christina Rossetti, the Oxford Movement, and *Goblin Market*', *Victorian Poetry*, 31/1 (1993), 79–93. Reads *Goblin Market* in the context of Tractarian theology and poetics.

—— 'Pilgrimage and Postponement: Christina Rossetti's *The Prince's Progress*', *Victorian Poetry*, 32/3–4 (1994), 279–98. The poem interpreted as principally concerned with the interpretation of symbolic events.

—— Harrison, Antony H., and Kooistra, Lorraine Janzen (eds.), *The Culture of Christina Rossetti: Female Poetics and Victorian Contexts* (Athens, Oh.: Ohio University Press, forthcoming). New essays on Christina Rossetti.

Auerbach, Nina, and Knoepflmacher, U. C. (eds.), *Forbidden Journeys: Fairy Tales and Fantasies by Victorian Women Writers* (Chicago: University of Chicago Press, 1992). Collection includes 'Nick', *Goblin Market*, and *Speaking Likenesses*, with reproductions of original illustrations.

Battiscombe, Georgina, *Christina Rossetti: A Divided Life* (London: Constable, 1981). Biography.

Bell, Mackenzie, *Christina Rossetti: A Biographical and Critical Study* (London: Hurst & Blackett, 1898). Important early study.

Bellas, Ralph A., *Christina Rossetti* (Boston: Twayne's English Author Series, 1977). One of a number of 1970s publications that signalled a resurgence of critical interest in Rossetti.

Belsey, Andrew, and Belsey, Catherine, 'Christina Rossetti: Sister to the Brotherhood', *Textual Practice*, 2/1 (1988), 30–50. Examines gender issues in relation to Rossetti and the PRB.

Bentley, D. M. R., 'The Meretricious and the Meritorious in *Goblin Market*: A Conjecture and an Analysis', in David A. Kent (ed.), *The Achievement of Christina Rossetti* (Ithaca, NY: Cornell University Press, 1987), 57–81. Reads *Goblin Market* in relation to contemporary religious and social contexts, including Rossetti's work at Highgate Penitentiary.

Blake, Kathleen, *Love and the Woman Question in Victorian Literature* (Brighton: Harvester, 1983). Includes some interesting commentary on Rossetti's 'self-postponement'.

Briggs, Julia, 'Women Writers and Writing for Children: From Sarah Fielding to E. Nesbit', in Gillian Avery and Julia Briggs (eds.), *Children and their Books* (Oxford: Clarendon Press, 1989), 221–50. Includes commentary on *Speaking Likenesses*.

Bristow, Joseph (ed.), *Victorian Women Poets* (Basingstoke: Macmillan, 1995). Collection of essays including several on Rossetti, listed individually in this bibliography.

—— '"No Friend Like a Sister": Christina Rossetti's Female Kin', *Victorian Poetry*, 33/2 (1995), 257–81. Examines the historical and cultural significance of Rossetti's representations of sisterhood.

Bump, Jerome, 'Christina Rossetti and the Pre-Raphaelite Brotherhood', in David A. Kent (ed.), *The Achievement of Christina Rossetti* (Ithaca, NY: Cornell University Press, 1987), 322–45.

Burlinson, Kathryn, '"All mouth and trousers": Christina Rossetti's Grotesque Bodies', in Isobel Armstrong and Virginia Blain (eds.), *Gender and Genre* (Basingstoke: Macmillan, 1998), ii. 292–312. Discusses representations of the body in the written and visual texts of *Speaking Likenesses*. The volume includes other new essays on Rossetti from the International Women's Poetry Conference, Birkbeck College, July 1995.

—— '"Frogs and fat toads": Christina Rossetti and the Significance of the Nonhuman', in Mary Arseneau *et al.* (ed.), *The Culture of Christina Rossetti* (Athens, Oh.: Ohio University Press, forthcoming). Explores Rossetti's ethical approach to nonhuman life.

Campbell, Elizabeth, 'Of Mothers and Merchants: Female Economics in Christina Rossetti's "Goblin Market"', *Victorian Studies*, 33/3 (1990), 393–410. Explores Rossetti's poetic responses to Victorian capitalism.

Cantalupo, Catherine Musello, 'Christina Rossetti: The Devotional Poet and the Rejection of Romantic Nature', in David A. Kent (ed.), *The Achievement of Christina Rossetti* (Ithaca, NY: Cornell University Press, 1987), 274–300. Argues that Rossetti's poetics fundamentally revise Romantic ideologies of nature.

Carpenter, Mary Wilson, '"Eat me, drink me, love me": The Consumable Female Body in Christina Rossetti's "Goblin Market"', *Victorian Poetry*, 29/4 (1991), 415–34. Reprinted in Cosslett (ed.),

Victorian Women Poets, 212–33.

Casey, Janet Galligani, 'The Potential of Sisterhood: Christina Rossetti's "Goblin Market"', *Victorian Poetry*, 29/1 (1991), 63–78.

Charles, Edna Kotin, *Christina Rossetti: Critical Perspectives, 1862–1982* (Selinsgrove, Pa.: Susquehanna University Press, 1985). Useful overview of trends in critical reception.

Cohen, Paula Marantz, 'Christina Rossetti's "Goblin Market": A Paradigm for Nineteenth-Century Anorexia Nervosa', *Hartford Studies in Literature*, 17, pt. 1 (1985), 1–18.

Conley, Susan, '"Poet's Right": Christina Rossetti as Anti-Muse and the Legacy of the "Poetess"', *Victorian Poetry*, 32/3–4 (1994), 365–86. Intertextual study of poems by Rossetti, Barrett Browning, and Michael Field.

Connor, Steven, '"Speaking Likenesses": Language and Repetition in Christina Rossetti's "Goblin Market"', *Victorian Poetry*, 22/4 (1984), 439–48. A brief but energetic and insightful essay informed by post-structuralist perspectives on language.

Cosslett, Tess (ed.), *Victorian Women Poets* (London: Longman, 1996). Reprints influential essays on Rossetti, cited individually in this bibliography.

Curran, Stuart, 'The Lyric Voice of Christina Rossetti', *Victorian Poetry*, 9 (1971), 287–99. Condemns Rossetti to the 'minor' rank of lyric poets. Critics have increasingly disagreed with this view.

D'Amico, Diane, 'Christina Rossetti: The Maturin Poems', *Victorian Poetry*, 19/2 (1981), 117–37. Examines the influence of Charles Maturin's gothic novels on a group of Rossetti's early poems.

—— 'Reading and Rereading George Herbert and Christina Rossetti', *John Donne Journal*, 4/2 (1985), 269–89. Compares poetic techniques used by the seventeenth-century poet and the influence of these on Rossetti's devotional poetry.

—— 'Eve, Mary, and Mary Magdalene: Christina Rossetti's Feminine Triptych', in David A. Kent (ed.), *The Achievement of Christina Rossetti* (Ithaca, NY: Cornell University Press, 1987), 175–91. Considers Rossetti's treatment of the three major female figures in Christian discourse.

—— 'Christina Rossetti's Christian Year: Comfort for the "Weary Heart"', *Victorian Newsletter*, 72 (1987), 36–42. Rossetti and Keble.

—— '"Equal Before God": Christina Rossetti and the Fallen Women of Highgate Penitentiary', in Antony H. Harrison and Beverley Taylor (eds.), *Gender and Discourse in Victorian Literature and Art* (De Kalb, Ill.: Northern Illinois University Press, 1992), 67–83. On Rossetti's involvement with Highgate.

—— 'Saintly Singer or Tanagra Figurine? Christina Rossetti Through the Eyes of Katharine Tynan and Sara Teasdale', *Victorian Poetry*, 32/3–4

(1994), 387–407. Examines Rossetti's influence on later women poets.

Denman, Kamilla, and Smith, Sarah, 'Christina Rossetti's Copy of C. B. Cayley's *Divine Comedy*', *Victorian Poetry*, 32/3–4 (1994), 315–38. Rossetti's relationship with Cayley examined via her annotations to his translation of Dante.

DeVitis, A. A., '*Goblin Market*: Fairy Tale and Reality', *Journal of Popular Culture*, 1, (1968), 418–26. Examines the fairy-tale elements in *Goblin Market*.

Edmond, Rod, *Affairs of the Hearth: Victorian Poetry and Domestic Narrative* (London: Routledge, 1988). Includes substantial discussion of *Goblin Market*.

Evans, B. Ifor, 'The Sources of Christina Rossetti's *Goblin Market*', *Modern Languages Review*, 28 (1933), 156–65. Early essay tracing literary influences on Rossetti's poem.

Finn, Mary E., *Writing the Incommensurable* (University Park, Pa.: Pennsylvania State University Press, 1992). Uses Kierkegaard's philosophical ideas to read Rossetti.

Flowers, Betty S., 'The Kingly Self: Rossetti as Woman Artist', in David A. Kent (ed.), *The Achievement of Christina Rossetti* (Ithaca, NY: Cornell University Press, 1987), 159–74. Focuses on gender issues raised in Rossetti's devotional poetry.

Garlick, Barbara, 'Christina Rossetti and the Gender Politics of Fantasy', in Kath Filmer (ed.), *The Victorian Fantasists* (Basingstoke: Macmillan, 1991), 133–52. Examines the conservative sexual politics in much Victorian fantasy art and considers *Goblin Market*'s subversions and revisions.

——— 'The Frozen Fountain: Christina Rossetti, the Virgin Model, and Youthful Pre-Raphaelitism', in Lloyd Davis (ed.), *Virginal Sexuality and Textuality in Victorian Literature* (Albany, NY: State University of New York, 1993), 105–27.

Gelpi, Barbara Charlesworth, '"Verses with a Good Deal about Sucking": Percy Bysshe Shelley and Christina Rossetti' in G. Kim Blank and Margot K. Louis (eds.), *Influence and Resistance in Nineteenth Century English Poetry* (Basingstoke: Macmillan, 1993), 150–65. Discusses the secular and religious significance of 'sucking' in *Goblin Market*.

Gilbert, Pamela, K., '"A Horrid Game": Woman as Social Entity in Christina Rossetti's Prose', *English: The Journal of the English Association*, 41/169 (1992), 1–23. Discusses *Speaking Likenesses* from a feminist perspective.

Gilbert, Sandra, and Gubar, Susan, *The Madwoman in the Attic* (New Haven: Yale University Press, 1979). Rossetti's work interpreted in the light of an aesthetic of renunciation. Extracts reprinted in Cosslett (ed.), *Victorian Women Poets*, 129–44.

Going, William, T., ' "Goblin Market" and the Pre-Raphaelite Brotherhood', *Pre-Raphaelite Review*, 3/1 (1979), 1–11.

Goldberg, Gail Lynn, 'Dante Gabriel Rossetti's "Revising Hand": His Illustrations for Christina Rossetti's Poems', *Victorian Poetry*, 20/3–4 (1982), 145–59.

Grass, Sean C., 'Nature's Perilous Variety in Rossetti's "Goblin Market"', *Nineteenth-Century Literature*, 51/3 (1996), 356–76.

Greer, Germaine, 'Introduction', in Christina Rossetti, *Goblin Market*, ed. Germaine Greer (New York: Stonehill Publishing, 1975).

Griffiths, Eric, 'The Disappointment of Christina G. Rossetti', *Essays in Criticism*, 47/2 (1997), 107–42.

Hanft, Lila, 'The Politics of Maternal Ambivalence in Christina Rossetti's *Sing-Song*', *Victorian Literature and Culture*, 19 (1991), 213–32.

Harrison, Antony H., *Christina Rossetti in Context* (Brighton: Harvester Press, 1988). Essential reading. Rossetti's major aesthetic influences thoroughly examined. Chapter reprinted in Cosslett (ed.), *Victorian Women Poets*, 176–93.

—— *Victorian Poets and Romantic Poems* (Charlottesville, Va.: University Press of Virginia, 1990). Includes chapter on Rossetti and Barrett Browning: 'In the Shadow of E. B. B.: Christina Rossetti and Ideological Estrangement'.

—— 'Christina Rossetti and the Sage Discourse of Feminist High Anglicanism', in Thaïs E. Morgan (ed.), *Victorian Sages and Cultural Discourse: Renegotiating Gender and Power* (New Brunswick, NJ: Rutgers University Press, 1990), 87–104. Considers Rossetti's challenges to Victorian gender ideologies in her devotional prose.

—— 'Christina Rossetti and the Romantics: Influence and Ideology', in G. Kim Blank and Margot K. Louis (eds.), *Influence and Resistance in Nineteenth Century English Poetry* (Basingstoke: Macmillan, 1993), 131–49. Examines Rossetti's overturning of Romantic secular ideologies.

—— (ed.), *Victorian Poetry*, 32/3–4 (1994). Special double issue on Rossetti. See *Victorian Poetry*.

—— (ed.), *The Letters of Christina Rossetti* (4 vols.; Charlottesville, Va.: University Press of Virginia, 1997–).

Helsinger, Elizabeth K., 'Consumer Power and the Utopia of Desire: Christina Rossetti's "Goblin Market"', *ELH*, 58/4 (1991), 903–33. Excellent essay on Victorian consumerism and Rossetti's treatment of women as both agents and objects in the Victorian economy. Reprinted in Bristow (ed.), *Victorian Women Poets*, 189–222.

Henwood, Dawn, 'Christian Allegory and Subversive Poetics: Christina Rossetti's *Prince's Progress* Re-examined', *Victorian Poetry*, 35/1 (1997), 83–94. Examines the poem's use of spiritual allegory and its challenge to social roles.

Hobbs, Colleen, 'A View from "The Lowest Place": Christina Rossetti's Devotional Prose', *Victorian Poetry*, 32/3–4 (1994), 409–28. Considers the problems and possibilities of reading Rossetti's devotional prose through a feminist lens.

Holt, Terrence, ' "Men sell not such in any town": Exchange in *Goblin Market*', *Victorian Poetry*, 28/1 (1990), 51–67. Examines the poem's language alongside that of the Victorian market economy. Reprinted in Cosslett (ed.), *Victorian Women Poets*, 194–211 and Leighton (ed.), *Victorian Women Poets: A Critical Reader*, 131–47.

Homans, Margaret, 'Syllables of Velvet: Dickinson, Rossetti and the Rhetorics of Sexuality', *Feminist Studies*, 11 (1985), 569–93. Reading influenced by French feminist and post-structuralist perspectives on language and sexuality.

Hönnighausen, Gisela, 'Emblematic Tendencies in the Works of Christina Rossetti', *Victorian Poetry*, 10/1 (1972), 1–15. One of the first post-war critics to draw attention to Rossetti's use of emblems.

Jones, Kathleen, *Learning Not to be First: The Life of Christina Rossetti* (Moreton-in-Marsh: Windrush Press, 1991). Little scholarly use; slight and poorly annotated.

Kaplan, Cora, 'The Indefinite Disclosed: Christina Rossetti and Emily Dickinson', in *Sea Changes* (London: Verso, 1986), 95–115. Psycho-analytically informed reading of poems including 'My Dream' and *Goblin Market*. Lively and insightful.

Katz, Wendy R., 'Muse From Nowhere: Christina Rossetti's Fantasy World in *Speaking Likenesses*', *Journal of Pre-Raphaelite Studies*, 4/1 (1984), 14–35. Reads Rossetti's fantasy stories against Lewis Carroll's; examines *Speaking Likenesses'* engagement with aggression and lecherousness.

Kent, David A. (ed.), *The Achievement of Christina Rossetti* (Ithaca, NY: Cornell University Press, 1987). Important collection of 1980s essays – recommended reading.

——' "By thought, word, and deed": George Herbert and Christina Rossetti', in Kent (ed.), *The Achievement of Christina Rossetti* (Ithaca, NY: Cornell University Press, 1987), 250–73. Traces connections between the two poets' techniques.

Knoepflmacher, U. C., 'Avenging Alice: Christina Rossetti and Lewis Carroll', *Nineteenth-Century Literature*, 41 (1986), 299–328. Argues that Rossetti's stories revise Carroll's worship of the female child.

Kooistra, Lorraine Janzen, 'The Representation of Violence/The Violence of Representation: Housman's Illustrations to Rossetti's *Goblin Market*', *English Studies in Canada*, 19/3 (1993), 305–28. Examines Housman's sexualized *fin de siècle* illustrations to the poem.

—— 'Modern Markets for *Goblin Market*', *Victorian Poetry*, 32/3–4 (1994), 249–77. Considers how the marketing of illustrated editions has shaped the poem's reception.

Leder, Sharon, and Abbott, Andrea, *The Language of Exclusion: The Poetry of Emily Dickinson and Christina Rossetti* (Contributions in Women's Studies, 83; New York: Greenwood Press, 1987). Less exciting than the title might suggest.

Leighton, Angela, '"When I am dead, my dearest": The Secret of Christina Rossetti', *Modern Philology*, 87 (1990), 373–88. Evocative exploration of the imagination at work in poems dwelling on death and the afterlife.

—— '"Because men made the laws": The Fallen Woman and the Woman Poet', *Victorian Poetry*, 27/2 (1989), 109–27. Reprinted in Bristow (ed.), *Victorian Women Poets*, 223–45, and Leighton (ed.), *Victorian Women Poets: A Critical Reader*, 215–34.

—— *Victorian Women Poets: Writing Against the Heart* (Hemel Hempstead: Harvester Wheatsheaf, 1992). Includes a fine chapter on Rossetti.

—— (ed.), *Victorian Women Poets: A Critical Reader* (Oxford: Basil Blackwell, 1996). Reprints key essays on Rossetti, cited individually in this bibliography.

McGann, Jerome J., 'Christina Rossetti's Poems: A New Edition and a Revaluation', *Victorian Studies*, 23 (1980), 237–54. Very influential in reassessment of poet's worth; also interprets history of twentieth-century critical responses. Reprinted in Leighton (ed.), *Victorian Women Poets: A Critical Reader*, 97–113.

—— 'The Religious Poetry of Christina Rossetti', *Critical Inquiry*, 10 (1983), 127–44. Historicizes the devotional poetry; argues Rossetti was drawn to doctrine of 'Soul Sleep'. Reprinted in Bristow (ed.), *Victorian Women Poets*, 167–88.

McGillis, Roderick, 'Simple Surfaces: Rossetti's Work for Children', in David A. Kent (ed.), *The Achievement of Christina Rossetti* (Ithaca, NY: Cornell University Press, 1987), 208–30. Discusses *Sing-Song* poems, *Goblin Market*, and *Speaking Likenesses*.

Marsh, Jan, *Christina Rossetti: A Literary Biography* (London: Jonathan Cape, 1994). Most important biography published in recent years. Highly informative about life, work, and literary contexts.

—— 'Christina Rossetti's Vocation: The Importance of *Goblin Market*', in *Victorian Poetry*, 32/3–4 (1994), 233–48. Concentrates on Rossetti's early career and the influences on her most famous poem.

Marshall, Linda E., 'What the Dead are Doing Underground: Hades and Heaven in the Writings of Christina Rossetti', *Victorian Newsletter*, 72 (1987), 55–60. Persuasively argues against Rossetti being preoccupied with 'Soul Sleep'.

—— '"Transfigured to His Likeness": Sensible Transcendentalism in Christina Rossetti's "Goblin Market"', *University of Toronto Quarterly*, 63 (1994), 429–50.

87

—— '"Abstruse the problems!": Unity and Divisions in Christina Rossetti's *Later Life: A Double Sonnet of Sonnets*', *Victorian Poetry*, 32/3–4 (1994), 299–314. Detailed reading of often neglected sonnet sequence.

Maxwell, Catherine, 'The Poetic Context of Christina Rossetti's "After Death"', *English Studies*, 76/2 (1995), 143–55. Focuses on Rossetti's subtle revisions of other texts and contexts in 'After Death'.

Mayberry, Katherine J., *Christina Rossetti and the Poetry of Discovery* (Baton Rouge, La.: Louisiana State University Press, 1989). Feminist monograph.

Mermin, Dorothy, 'Heroic Sisterhood in *Goblin Market*', *Victorian Poetry*, 21/2 (1983), 107–18. Widely read feminist essay on Rossetti's representations of sisterhood. Reprinted in Cosslett (ed.), *Victorian Women Poets*, 145–57.

Michie, Helena, 'There is no Friend Like a Sister: Sisterhood as Sexual Difference', *ELH*, 56 (1989), 401–22.

Montefiore, Jan, *Feminism and Poetry* (London: Pandora, 1987). Includes discussion of 'Monna Innominata' and 'The heart knoweth its own bitterness'.

Morrill, David F., '"Twilight is not good for Maidens": Uncle Polidori and the Psychodynamics of Vampirism in *Goblin Market*', *Victorian Poetry*, 28/1 (1990), 1–16. Despite suggestive title, not a persuasive essay.

Norton, Caroline, '"The Angel in the House" and "The Goblin Market"', *Macmillan's Magazine*, 8 (Sept. 1863), 401–2.

Packer, Lona Mosk, *Christina Rossetti* (Berkeley and Los Angeles: University of California Press, 1963). Biography. Despite wealth of information and commentary, flawed by its now discredited thesis that Rossetti was in love with William Bell Scott.

Peterson, Linda H., 'Restoring the Book: The Typological Hermeneutics of Christina Rossetti and the PRB', in *Victorian Poetry*, 32/3–4 (1994), 209–32. Discusses Rossetti's challenging uses of typology in *Goblin Market* and 'The Prince's Progress'; the latter read against Bunyan's *Pilgrim's Progress*.

Proctor, Ellen, *A Brief Memoir of Christina Rossetti* (London: SPCK, 1895).

Psomiades, Kathy Alexis, 'Feminine and Poetic Privacy in Christina Rossetti's "Autumn" and "A Royal Princess"', *Victorian Poetry*, 31/2 (1993), 187–202.

Rosenblum, Dolores, 'Christina Rossetti's Religious Poetry: Watching Looking, Keeping Vigil', *Victorian Poetry*, 20/1 (1982), 33–50. An interesting essay on Anglican women's devotional practices and the dynamics of vision in Rossetti's poetry. Reprinted in Leighton (ed.), *Victorian Women Poets: A Critical Reader*, 114–30.

—— *Christina Rossetti: The Poetry of Endurance* (Carbondale, Ill.: Southern Illinois University Press, 1986). Important feminist monograph focusing on Rossetti's construction of a poetic identify that resists and revises patriarchal literary traditions.

—— 'Christina Rossetti and Poetic Sequence', in David A. Kent (ed.), *The Achievement of Christina Rossetti* (Ithaca, NY: Cornell University Press, 1987), 132–56. Demonstrates the significance of Rossetti's ordering of poems in her collections.

Sagan, Miriam, ' "Goblin Market" and Feminist Literary Criticism', *Pre-Raphaelite Review*, 3/2 (1980), 66–76. Reviews early feminist criticism.

Schofield, Linda, 'Being and Understanding: Devotional Poetry of Christina Rossetti and the Tractarians', in David A. Kent (ed.), *The Achievement of Christina Rossetti* (Ithaca, NY: Cornell University Press, 1987), 301–21. Argues that Rossetti develops and personalizes Tractarian poetics.

Shalkhauser, Marian, 'The Feminine Christ', *Victorian Newsletter*, 10 (1957), 19–20. Notes Rossetti's use of a feminine Christ-figure in *Goblin Market*.

Shaw, W. David, 'Poet of Mystery: The Art of Christina Rossetti', in David A. Kent (ed.), *The Achievement of Christina Rossetti* (Ithaca, NY: Cornell University Press, 1987), 23–56. Subtle close reading exploring poetic strategies by which Rossetti conjures a sense of mystery and the ineffable.

Sickbert, Virginia, 'Christina Rossetti and Victorian Children's Poetry: A Maternal Challenge to the Patriarchal Family', *Victorian Poetry*, 31/4 (1993), 385–410. Discusses *Sing-Song*.

Smulders, Sharon, ' "A Form that Differences": Vocational Metaphors in the Poetry of Christina Rossetti and Gerard Manley Hopkins', *Victorian Poetry*, 29/2 (1991), 161–73.

—— 'Woman's Enfranchisement in Christina Rossetti's Poetry', *Texas Studies in Literature*, 34/4 (1992), 568–88.

—— 'Sound, Sense and Structure in Christina Rossetti's *Sing-Song*', *Children's Literature*, 22 (1994), 3–26.

Stanwood, P. G., 'Christina Rossetti's Devotional Prose', in David A. Kent (ed.), *The Achievement of Christina Rossetti* (Ithaca, NY: Cornell University Press, 1987), 231–49.

Stone, Marjorie, 'Sisters in Art: Christina Rossetti and Elizabeth Barrett Browning', *Victorian Poetry*, 32/3–4 (1994), 339–64. Intertextual study of the two poets.

Swann, Thomas Burnett, *Wonder and Whimsy: The Fantastic World of Christina Rossetti* (Francestown, NH: Marshall Jones, 1960). Useful introductory reading for Rossetti's use of fantasy modes, but study is limited in approach and analysis.

Tennyson, G. B., *Victorian Devotional Poetry: The Tractarian Mode* (Cambridge, Mass.: Harvard University Press, 1981). Includes substantial discussion of Tractarian influences on Rossetti's devotional poetry.

Thomas, Frances, *Christina Rossetti* (London: Virago, 1994). Biography.

Thompson, Deborah Ann, 'Anorexia as a Lived Trope: Christina Rossetti's "Goblin Market"', *Mosaic*, 24, pts. 3–4 (1992), 89–106.

Victorian Poetry, 32/3–4 (1994), ed. Antony H. Harrison. Special double issue celebrating Rossetti's centennial. Contains Introduction and ten essays on Rossetti. Highly recommended.

Waller, John O., 'Christ's Second Coming: Christina Rossetti and the Premillenialist William Dodsworth', *Bulletin of the New York Public Library*, 73 (1969), 465–82.

Watson, Jeanie, '"Men Sell Not Such in any Town": Christina Rossetti's Goblin Fruit of Fairy Tale', *Children's Literature*, 12 (1984), 61–77. Examines fairy-tale aspects of *Goblin Market*.

―――― '"Eat Me, Drink Me, Love Me": The Dilemma of Sisterly Self-Sacrifice', *Journal of Pre-Raphaelite Studies*, 7, pt. 1 (1986), 50–62.

Weathers, Winston, 'Christina Rossetti: The Sisterhood of Self', *Victorian Poetry*, 3/2 (1965), 81–9. Important early essay; argues that Rossetti's representations of women may be read as externalized aspects of the self.

Westerholm, Joel, '"I Magnify Mine Office": Christina Rossetti's Authoritative Voice in her Devotional Prose', *Victorian Newsletter*, 84 (1993), 11–17.

Whitla, William, 'Questioning the Convention: Christina Rossetti's Sonnet Sequence "Monna Innominata"', in David A. Kent (ed.), *The Achievement of Christina Rossetti* (Ithaca, NY: Cornell University Press, 1987), 82–131. Close reading of sonnet sequence.

Williams, Linda Ruth, *Critical Desire: Psychoanalysis and the Literary Subject* (London: Edward Arnold, 1995). Includes discussion of Rossetti, masochism, and the uncanny in chapter entitled '"A Short Way by a Long Wandering": Writing the Death Drive', pp. 154–85.

Woolf, Virginia, *The Common Reader, Second Series* (London: Hogarth Press, 1965), 237–44. Includes Woolf's essay, 'I am Christina Rossetti'.

―――― *A Writer's Diary*, ed. Leonard Woolf (London: Hogarth Press, 1969). Entry for 5 Aug. 1918 includes comments on Rossetti's art and faith.

OTHER WORKS MENTIONED IN THE TEXT

Apter, T. E., *Fantasy Literature* (Basingstoke: Macmillan, 1982).

Arnold, Matthew, *The Complete Prose Works of Matthew Arnold*, i, ed. R. H. Super (Ann Arbor: University of Michigan Press, 1960).

Bakhtin, Mikhail, *Problems of Dostoevsky's Poetics*, trans. R. W. Rotsel (Ann Arbor: Ardis, 1973).

Barkan, Leonard, *The Gods Made Flesh: Metamorphosis and the Pursuit of*

Paganism (New Haven: Yale University Press, 1986).

Barrett Browning, Elizabeth, *Aurora Leigh*, ed. Cora Kaplan (London: The Women's Press, 1978).

Brontë, Emily, *The Complete Poems of Emily Jane Brontë*, ed. C. W. Hatfield (New York: Columbia University Press, 1948).

Carroll, Lewis, *The Annotated Snark*, ed. Martin Gardner (Harmondsworth: Penguin, 1962).

Carter, Angela, *Nothing Sacred* (London: Virago, 1982).

Dickens, Charles, 'Frauds on the Fairies', *Household Words*, 8/184 (5 Oct. 1853), 58–62.

Dickinson, Emily, *Emily Dickinson: The Complete Poems*, ed. Thomas H. Johnson (London: Faber & Faber, 1970).

Freud, Sigmund, *Introductory Lectures on Psychoanalysis* (1916; Pelican Freud, 1; Harmondsworth: Penguin, 1973; repr. 1991).

—— *The Interpretation of Dreams* (1900; Pelican Freud, 4; Harmondsworth: Penguin, 1976; repr. 1991).

—— *Jokes and their Relation to the Unconscious* (1905; Pelican Freud, 6; Harmondsworth: Penguin, 1976; repr. 1991).

Keble, John, 'Sacred Poetry', *Quarterly Review*, 32 (1825), 211–32.

—— *Lectures on Poetry, 1832–1841*, ii, trans. Edward Kershaw Francis (Oxford: Clarendon Press, 1912).

Keightley, Thomas, *The Fairy Mythology* (London, 1828).

Kristeva, Julia, *The Kristeva Reader*, ed. Toril Moi (Oxford: Basil Blackwell, 1986).

Lecercle, Jean-Jacques, *Philosophy of Nonsense* (London: Routledge, 1994).

Maclaren, Archibald, *The Fairy Family* (London: 1857).

Phillips, Adam, *On Flirtation* (London: Faber & Faber, 1994).

Rich, Adrienne, 'Compulsory Heterosexuality and Lesbian Existence', *Signs*, 5/4 (1980), 631–60.

Shrimpton, Nicholas, 'New Spirits of the Age', *TLS*, 6 Feb. 1998, p. 6.

Tigges, Wim, *An Anatomy of Literary Nonsense* (Amsterdam: Rodopi, 1988).

Truax, Elizabeth, *Metamorphosis in Shakespeare's Plays* (Lampeter: Edwin Mellen Press, 1992).

Warner, Marina, *From the Beast to the Blonde* (1994; repr. London: Vintage, 1995).

Zipes, Jack, *Breaking the Magic Spell: Radical Theories of Folk and Fairy Tales* (1979; repr. London: Routledge, 1992).

Index